the Marginal Teacher

THIRD EDITION

the Marginal Teacher

A Step-by-Step Guide
to Fair Procedures for Identification
and Dismissal

C. Edward Lawrence
Myra K. Vachon
Donald O. Leake
Brenda H. Leake

THIRD EDITION

CORWIN PRESS
A Sage Publications Company
Thousand Oaks, California

For information:

Corwin Press
A Sage Publications Company
2455 Teller Road
Thousand Oaks, California 91320
www.corwinpress.com

Sage Publications Ltd.
1 Oliver's Yard
55 City Road
London EC1Y 1SP
United Kingdom

Sage Publications India Pvt. Ltd.
B-42, Panchsheel Enclave
Post Box 4109
New Delhi 110 017 India

Printed in the United States of America.

Library of Congress Cataloging-in-Publication Data

Lawrence, C. Edward.
The marginal teacher: A step-by-step guide to fair procedures for identification and dismissal / C. Edward Lawrence.—3rd ed.
     p. cm.
Rev. ed. of: The marginal teacher. c2000.
Includes bibliographical references and index.
ISBN 1-4129-1473-6 (cloth) — ISBN 1-4129-1474-4 (pbk.)
   1. Teachers—Rating of—United States. 2. Teachers—Dismissal of—United States.
I. Marginal teacher. II. Title.
LB2838.M376 2005
371.14′4—dc22   2004025337

This book is printed on acid-free paper.

05   06   07   08   09   10   9   8   7   6   5   4   3   2   1

Acquisitions Editor:	Elizabeth Brenkus
Editorial Assistant:	Candice L. Ling
Production Editor:	Laureen A. Shea
Typesetter:	C&M Digitals (P) Ltd.
Proofreader:	Colleen Brennan
Indexer:	Pamela Van Huss
Cover Designer:	Michael Dubowe
Graphic Designer:	Lisa Miller

Contents

List of Sample Resource Documents

A Cautionary Note

This guidebook is not a legal document. It is intended to provide accurate information about the subject area. It is sold with the understanding that the publisher and the author are not engaged in rendering legal or other professional services. Specifically, the recommendations contained herein are guidelines only and not legal advice, and the publisher and the author do not warrant, in any manner, their suitability for any particular usage. If legal advice or other expert assistance is required, the services of an attorney or other competent professional, with knowledge of all laws pertaining to the reader and the jurisdiction, should be sought.

Preface

During his first year as a middle school principal, the author learned the hard way how frustrating and difficult it can be to terminate an ineffective teacher. Even the most experienced school administrators struggle with this task. This book is designed to guide school administrators, supervisors, district office personnel responsible for evaluations, and university graduate students through the complicated teacher dismissal process. Over the course of several years, resources compiled by the author took the shape of a manuscript or guide to help principals and supervisors avoid the same pitfalls the author encountered while going through the process of terminating a teacher. The author believed his experience and resources would benefit other professionals who are involved in supervising teachers. Subsequently, the first edition of *The Marginal Teacher: A Step-by-Step Guide to Fair Procedures for Identification and Dismissal* was published in 1993 to support principals and supervisors throughout the cumbersome teacher dismissal process. Throughout the years, this book has helped many principals navigate through the complicated teacher evaluation process. Principals must do their homework in order to conduct an effective teacher dismissal. Poorly prepared documentation will result in the dismissal being overturned by a school board, appeals board, arbitrator, or other ruling body. This book illustrates actions the principal can integrate into the evaluation process to successfully gather documentation to terminate an ineffective teacher. It provides numerous tools to help streamline the teacher evaluation process— sample letters, observation forms, a calendar with action dates identified, and a sample unsatisfactory evaluation binder. You can modify these resource documents to fit your effort to create a strong case for the termination of an ineffective teacher.

The Marginal Teacher is predicated upon seven basic assumptions about a school district's evaluation system. First, that the district school committee has designated improved student achievement as its number one priority. Second, the school district does not use a portfolio or a Peer Review Program to evaluate teachers. Third, the principal has followed the legal and contractual obligations of the master contract, school district policies, and state laws relative to the teacher evaluation process. Fourth, the principal understands the physical and psychological demands of the teacher dismissal process. Fifth, the principal has established and implemented consistent teacher evaluation procedures. Sixth, the principal has established administrative and instructional credibility with the staff to analyze and describe what is occurring in the teacher's classroom to diagnose the causes of the unsatisfactory teaching. Seventh, the principal has discussed the teacher dismissal process with individuals in central administration as well as the attorney for the school district to obtain their support and to ensure that legal and contractual obligations are met.

This book correlates with two other guidebooks—*How to Handle Staff Misconduct* and *The Incompetent Specialists*—that may point the principal in the right direction to prepare an unsatisfactory teacher evaluation. However, these books are not necessarily the perfect models of the teacher dismissal process or of the best strategies to employ. Accordingly, before using this or any other guide, carefully review your district's teacher evaluation procedures and related stipulations contained within your state statutes, school district policies, and the master contract.

Chapter 1 is an introduction to the teacher evaluation process that explains the due process requirements. Chapter 2 explains the types of behavior that are considered misconduct and the steps in the teacher appraisal process. Chapter 3 describes the marginal teacher, the good teacher, a schematic view of the basic steps in the teacher evaluation process, and the role of the evaluators. Chapter 4 explains the opening procedures for starting the school year to include regular and constructive conduct observations of all teachers. Chapter 5 explains how to create an organized binder containing the documentation that a principal may need to support an unsatisfactory evaluation. Chapter 6 explains how to successfully prepare to conduct observations of all teachers. This chapter also includes the steps of conducting pre- and postobservation conferences and sample informal and formal observation forms, memoranda of concerns, and letters that document the guidance and assistance provided to the teacher. A new evaluation instrument, the Memorandum of Accomplishment, was added to give the principal another strategy to follow up on the first Memorandum of Concerns. Chapter 7 details how to implement an intensive teacher assistance plan. Chapter 8 is designed to prepare the principal for the important school-level dismissal meeting. Chapter 9 is a new chapter that explains how to successfully conduct a school-level meeting and includes a sample narrative to use to present the case. Chapter 10 is a new chapter that explains how to effectively present the unsatisfactory evaluation at the district-level conference to an impartial hearing officer and school committee—a decision about the teacher's future employment in the school district is made at this step. The following resources can be found at the end of the book for easy reference: A has letters to the principal's supervisor; B is a calendar with a suggested action timeline; C is a summary of state-by-state teacher evaluation statutes; and D is the Sample Unsatisfactory Teacher Evaluation Documentation, including a full Sample Unsatisfactory Teacher Evaluation Binder that will come in especially handy as a reference while reading Chapter 9. Please note that all forms, sample letters, and the full Sample Unsatisfactory Teacher Evaluation Documentation can be found on the dual-format CD-ROM included in the back of the book. Forms can be downloaded and easily customized for your own needs in assembling documentation to support an unsatisfactory evaluation.

Acknowledgments

I sincerely thank those principals, assistant principals, deans, and supervisors who offered their insightful suggestions to this guide to dismissing an ineffective teacher. I want to especially thank Dr. Myra K. Vachon, who was the coauthor for the first and second editions. I am also thankful to Lemmie D., my wife and critical friend, for her review of this document. Finally, I extend thanks to Corwin Press staff: original contact person, Gracia Alkema, past president, who gave me support and encouragement for two decades; Elizabeth Brenkus, my current Acquisitions Editor; Robert D. Clouse, Editorial Director; Douglas Rife, President; and members of the Corwin Press team who followed this book from the editorial through the production stage. A special thanks goes to Cheryl Williams who formatted the text, tables, figures, and schematic view.

The author and Corwin Press gratefully acknowledge the contributions of the following individuals:

Thomas Alsbury, Assistant Professor
Educational Leadership
    and Policy Studies
Iowa State University
Ames, IA

Albert Armer, Principal
Wortham Elementary School
Wortham, TX

Edgar Gill, Associate Professor
School of Education and Behavioral
    Studies
Azusa Pacific University
Azusa, CA

Dennis McKnight, Principal
Wissahickon High School
Ambler, PA

Jenny Mudgett, Principal
Caldwell Elementary School
Auburndale, FL

Paul Young, Principal/Corwin Author
West Elementary School
Lancaster, OH

About the Author

C. Edward Lawrence, president of the Lawrence Educational Consulting Group, has advised many school districts on how to prepare and win unsatisfactory staff member evaluation and misconduct cases. Dr. Lawrence has nearly 30 years of experience in the field of education—he has served as a teacher, principal, assistant superintendent, author, and professor. For the past nine years, Dr. Lawrence has inspired future educators as a Clinical Professor in the Department of Curriculum and Instruction at the University of Nevada, Las Vegas. He earned a bachelor's degree in elementary education from West Virginia State University, a master's degree in guidance and counseling from Marquette University, a certificate in administrative leadership, and a PhD in urban education from the University of Wisconsin-Milwaukee. Before holding his current position, he was the assistant superintendent for a large urban school district, in which he had an extensive educational career in public education. He served as a teacher, counselor, team leader, and assistant principal at the elementary, middle, and high school levels, as principal at the elementary and middle school levels, as director of alternative programs, and as a community superintendent. In addition, he served as a hearing officer for unsatisfactory teacher evaluations, second-step misconduct, and immediate teacher suspensions. He was an adjunct instructor in the Department of Administrative Leadership, teaching courses in clinical supervision and critical issues, including staff misconduct and evaluating the marginal teacher. Dr. Lawrence is author of the following books: *The Marginal Teacher: A Step-by-Step Guide to Fair Procedures for Identification and Dismissal* (1993; the second edition was published in 2001); *How to Handle Staff Misconduct: A Step-by-Step Guide* (1995; the second edition was published in 2003); and *The Incompetent Specialist: How to Evaluate, Document Performance, and Dismiss School Staff* (1996).

1

Preparing for the Teacher Evaluation Process

Successfully preparing for the teacher evaluation process requires an understanding of why few teachers are terminated, how principals stay away from the appraisal process, provisions in the master contract, terminating nontenured and tenured teachers, and upholding the teacher's dismissal. Few teachers across the nation are terminated for incompetence or resign due to unsatisfactory teaching. In fact, in many school districts, less than one percent of the total teaching staff is terminated for incompetence. Unfortunately, countless numbers of principals are too apprehensive and lack the confidence and skills to assemble the documentation to recommend a teacher's dismissal based on incompetence. Some principals are too sympathetic to criticize a teacher's unsatisfactory teaching or do not have the fortitude to recommend the firing of a teacher. Accordingly, they protect these deficient teachers by taking no steps to terminate them, and instead, allow them to transfer to other schools. Consequently, at the beginning of each school year, the "dance of the lemons" or "passing of the trash or bad apples" occurs where thousands of bad teachers are transferred from one school to another. Sadly, these substandard teachers transfer from school to school, continuing their ineffective teaching until they decide to quit or resign. As a result, principals continue to face the frustrating task of evaluating ineffective veteran teachers who have received satisfactory evaluations over the years. These frustrated principals may blame their fellow principals or their supervisors (the superintendent, the school committee, or the school district attorney) for the complicated teacher dismissal process.

Principals Stay Away From the Teacher Dismissal Process

Principals use various strategies to avoid the complicated teacher dismissal process. A number of principals will instead employ other tactics to discourage deficient teachers, such as eliminating the teacher's assistant to make the job more complicated, reassigning a special program, or changing the teacher's schedule to a less attractive schedule—which could mean a grade-level change and an increase in class preparation. Other principals will discontinue an educational program or incorporate a subject that the teacher is unlicensed to teach in hopes that this will force the teacher to transfer to another school.

Some principals will tolerate incompetent teachers for the entire school year as long as parent or student complaints are kept to a minimum. At the end of the school year, the principal will harshly threaten the teachers with unsatisfactory evaluations if they plan to return the next school year. As a result, the teachers, fearful of losing their jobs, will transfer to other schools to continue unsuccessfully teaching, and the problem continues. Principals may be happy that incompetent teachers transfer to other schools but soon discover that the cycle continues when new ineffective teachers transfer into their schools.

Another way principals get around the difficult evaluation process is to encourage the ineffective teacher to take a medical or sabbatical leave with the anticipation that the teacher will retire at the end of the leave. Many of these teachers do not resign but quietly transfer to another school and the "dance of the lemons" goes on.

Some principals are so fearful of the teacher evaluation process that they will transfer to another school. They disapprove of the teachers' association taking an aggressive stance to keep the ineffective teacher in the classroom. A principal might feel that it is easier to transfer to another school than to be caught up in the dismissal and grievance hassles. Nevertheless, a principal's foremost responsibility is to make sure that only the best teachers are on the job at his or her school, and that includes taking the necessary steps to effectively prove that a deficient teacher should be terminated from the school district.

Master Contract Provisions

A number of contracts have imprudent and ridiculous evaluation provisions entrenched in a chunky master contract, making it nearly impossible for the principal to recommend a teacher's dismissal. These evaluation provisions are supported by complicated arbitration rulings that further compound the teacher dismissal process. For instance, if teachers receive unsatisfactory evaluations for two years in a row, they must remain at the school for three years to get remedial assistance. Principals could push ineffective teachers to transfer to another school or they could retain them and work on improving teaching skills. A busy principal does not have time in the school day to work with deficient teachers to improve their teaching skills. A *wise* principal would give the ineffective teacher a satisfactory evaluation to avoid the dismissal process and then apply pressure to force the teacher to transfer to another school.

Sadly, more than 50 percent of the students in a certain school district read below grade level; one in four third graders yearly fails the state assessment tests or fails to meet federal academic standards. The student population is plagued by high drop-out and suspension rates and low attendance and graduation rates. Unless the unsatisfactory (U-rating) evaluation provisions are negotiated out of the master contract, principals in this school district will continue thinking it is impossible to terminate a bad teacher. This school district and the teacher's association will continue to engage in open public arguments to attract attention by giving out ambiguous information about the evaluation provisions in the teacher contract. In addition, state lawmakers and district or federal courts are reluctant to intervene into a contractual agreement unless there are unlawful constitutional right infringements. Possibly the only chance for a principal to get around the provisions blocking termination of ineffective teachers is if the teachers fail basic-skills examinations or federally mandated testing, which proves that they are not highly qualified in the subject area or in some other way fail to meet state license criteria.

Terminating Tenured and Nontenured Teachers

Many principals have been told that tenure guarantees teachers lifelong teaching positions unless they are involved in criminal misconduct. In reality, both nontenured and tenured teachers can be terminated for unsatisfactory teaching. The principal is not required to compile extensive documentation to prove the *nontenured teacher* is unsatisfactory. Therefore, the principal and other evaluators must aggressively evaluate nontenured individuals for the first three years to make sure that deficient teachers are terminated before they gain tenure. In addition, principals must support each other by writing negative comments on the teacher's yearly evaluation form so that the next evaluator can use these comments to help prove the teacher is unsatisfactory. There is usually no formal board hearing to terminate a nontenured teacher; only board approval is typically required. A tenured teacher can be terminated, but it takes more work to compile the documentation to support and back up the dismissal. A principal needs to conduct numerous classroom observations, intervene to assess the teacher's performance, make improvement suggestions, provide assistance, and set a precise date for the teacher to demonstrate satisfactory performance improvement. A hearing must be held with the school committee to decide the teacher's future employment with the school district. If the committee votes to terminate the teacher, the Human Resources Department will notify the teacher in writing. If the teacher disagrees with the committee's decision, an appeal may be filed with an arbitrator according to the contract.

Nonunion School Districts

Many state statutes do not authorize school districts to engage in collective bargaining with teachers. For these nonunion school districts, the state board of education may be responsible for outlining procedures for the local educational agencies (LEA) to implement the course of action for the teacher evaluation. For example, the steps in the evaluation process may consist of interviews (oral or written), several formal observations, an intensive assistance plan for the teacher, and a year-end summative evaluation. The summative steps in the teacher dismissal may include a meeting with the principal, a hearing with a district hearing officer, a school board hearing, and a grievance process to appeal an adverse decision. Although some school districts may have several teacher organizations, teachers are entitled to be represented by their association or legal representatives of their choice throughout union evaluation process. Whether the school district is nonunion or union, every principal must meet just cause standards when considering teacher dismissal.

Upholding the Teacher Dismissal

Even if you think that you have a good case to terminate an ineffective teacher, you can never predict the outcome nor should you believe that it is a slam-dunk case. It is impossible to have a 100 percent guarantee that a teacher will be terminated. If you can answer "yes" to the following due process questions, the probability is great that the case for dismissal is strong:

1. Did all teachers working at the school(s) know the evaluation process for the school district?

2. Was the evaluation process consistently applied to all teachers?

3. Was the teacher treated consistently with other teachers?

4. Was the teacher singled out?

5. Did the observations include all phases of the teacher's assignment, morning and afternoon?

6. Was there a continuous and accurately dated file of all conferences with and observations of the teacher?

7. Did the teacher receive written memoranda of concerns specifying exact deficiencies?

8. In each memorandum of concerns given to the teacher, did the teacher receive a list of specific suggestions for correcting deficiencies and ways to achieve a satisfactory level of performance?

9. Was an intensive assistance plan established and implemented for the teacher using school and district resources?

10. Was the teacher given a reasonable period to improve teaching performance?

11. Was the teacher informed in writing that failure to achieve an acceptable level of performance improvement by a specified date would result in the assurance of an unsatisfactory evaluation?

You must carefully review these just cause standards throughout the dismissal process to make sure that the teacher dismissal is not haphazard, unreasonable, or improper to protect yourself and your district against a discrimination lawsuit based on age, gender, race, religion, or sexual orientation.

Words of Wisdom

During the teacher dismissal process, anxiety runs high between the principal and the teacher, and an indiscreet expression of opinion repeated out of context can create chaos. Above all, you must resist temptation to talk about the teacher evaluation process with other staff members in the building, especially where the dismissal process is taking place. Specifically, do not speak off the record to media or other individuals about the case. Always remember that the dismissal is a highly confidential matter between you and the respective teacher. In addition, you should avoid social relationships with any staff members and only choose confidantes outside the school environment. Accordingly, stay away from social gatherings with staff members, especially those that may involve drinking alcohol at house parties or going to bars after work hours. As a final point, never become romantically involved with a staff member, especially if you are married. This situation detracts from your ability to conduct school business in a professional manner, and rumors circulating around the school may potentially explode in the media during the dismissal hearings. Stated as empathetically as possible—value your professional reputation as a role model for students, parents, and staff, and uphold high standards in the community by showing respect for your spouse, children, and family.

Understanding Misconduct and the Teacher Appraisal Process

Comprehensive and accurate performance appraisals are critical components of the teacher dismissal process. Principals must understand the role of individuals involved in the appraisal process, the steps of a complete appraisal, and how the definition of misconduct applies to the dismissal. Misconduct includes inappropriate staff member conduct, including:

- Unexcused absences and tardiness
- Neglect of duty
- Using abusive, insulting, degrading, and/or profane language
- Using corporal punishment
- Insubordination
- Unethical or incorrect administering of assessment tests
- Sexual misconduct
- Abuse of controlled substances
- Theft and fraud
- Computer misuse with criminal intent
- Criminal misconduct outside the school setting
- Conduct unbecoming an educator

As the principal, you must put into writing the acceptable standards of conduct for all staff members at work. Staff members must be warned that they are subject to disciplinary action up to and including dismissal for violating the acceptable standards of conduct at work. The teacher evaluation appraises the competency of the teacher to determine if he or she is teaching at a satisfactory level. Essex (2004) defines incompetence to include inefficiency, lack of skill, inadequate knowledge of subject matter, inability or unwillingness to teach the curricula, failure to work effectively with colleagues and parents, failure to maintain discipline, inadequate management of the classroom, and attitudinal deficiencies (p. 252). This book supports Essex's incompetence definition to describe the marginal teacher.

Teacher Evaluators

The principal coordinates the teacher evaluation process, issues letters relative to the evaluation process, maintains the documentation, and presents at the unsatisfactory evaluation meeting, conference, and school committee hearing. The assistant principal/dean makes observations, provides assistance, and supplements the support given to the teacher. The curriculum supervisor has expertise in the teacher's area of certification to provide the teacher support and assistance. The mentor (coach) assists the teacher but usually is not permitted by the bargaining unit/association to provide evaluative statements about the teacher or testify at unsatisfactory evaluation hearings except as part of a Peer Review Program. However, a statement from the mentor (coach) regarding the dates, times, and the extent to which assistance was provided would be appropriate and admissible. Finally, the district curriculum supervisor will become involved in the teacher's evaluation if an intensive assistance plan is a part of the district's evaluation procedure. All evaluators must work within the contractual and legal constraints of the evaluation process.

A Schematic View of the Teacher Evaluation Process

Following is a 12-step overview of the teacher evaluation process (also see Figure 2.1). Step 1 requires principals to know the legal guidelines. Steps 2 and 3 are related to the communication of the evaluation procedures and the standards for performance. Steps 4 and 5 discuss the scheduling and completion of formal classroom observations. Steps 6 and 7 outline how to provide feedback and guidance to teachers throughout the appraisal process. Steps 8 through 12 relate to teachers who fail to improve their performance. Specifically, steps 8 through 11 pertain to the different levels of teacher dismissal hearings, and step 12 details the appeals process for dissatisfied teachers. Although some variations naturally occur in school district evaluation procedures, you should follow this procedure to create a successful teacher dismissal case.

Steps in the Teacher Evaluation Process

Step 1   Study the teacher evaluation provisions in your state statutes, master contract, and written district standards. The state statutes put in plain language the cause for a teacher's dismissal: attendance, planning, instructional methods, classroom management, subject matter competency, or failure to complete a satisfactory remediation plan.

Step 2   Inform all teachers about the evaluation procedures within the first 30 days of the school year. This could occur at a regular staff meeting,

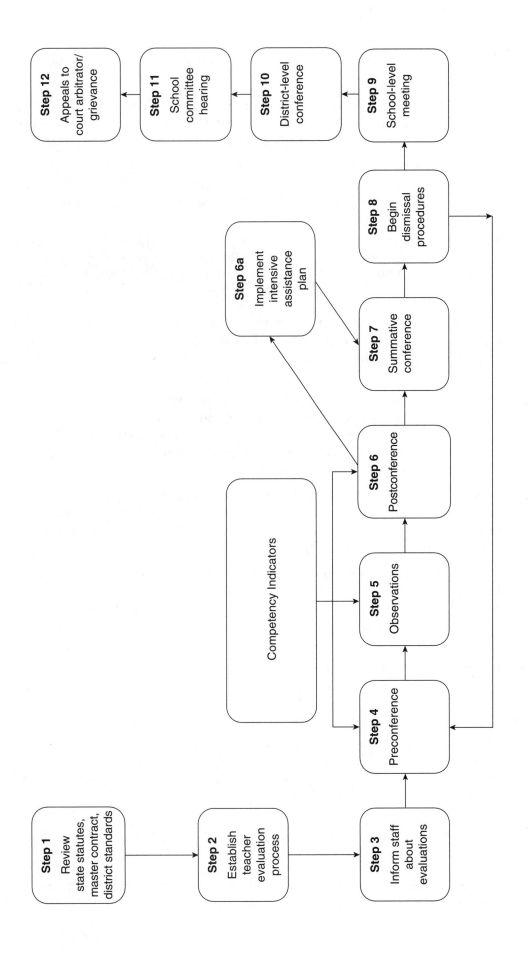

Figure 2.1 A Schematic View of the Teacher Evaluation Process

through information printed in the staff handbook, or in a separate memorandum.

Step 3   Identify the teacher's evaluator in a memorandum, explain the evaluation procedures, and attach evaluation instruments using district standards and a copy of the evaluation section from the master contract.

Step 4   Hold a preconference with tenured and nontenured teachers to plan the day and time to conduct formal observations. (The first formal observation is announced, and the others are unannounced during the morning or afternoon.)

Step 5   Conduct formal teacher observations for the duration of the class period or at least 30–45 minutes to collect measurable information. If the lesson plan is short, use two observations to complete the teacher assessment.

Step 6   Hold a feedback meeting within five school days after the observation. Focus on the teacher's strengths and weaknesses and follow up the meeting by sending a memorandum of concerns or letter summarizing the meeting.

Step 6a   Create a plan of intensive assistance for teachers in need of improvement. Continue observations, compile documentation, and issue a letter to place the teacher on notice of a potential unsatisfactory teacher evaluation. If the teacher does not improve, you must start the dismissal process in January and February.

Step 7   Hold summative teacher evaluation conferences in April and May to provide teaching improvement suggestions. Complete the teacher evaluation form, submit a copy to the Human Resources Department, and keep a copy for the school file.

Step 8   Begin the dismissal procedures. Follow the master contract stipulations related to the school meeting, district meeting, and school committee hearing. Prepare for the unsatisfactory evaluation meetings, complete the unsatisfactory evaluation form, and organize the documentation in a binder.

Step 9   Conduct a school-level dismissal meeting.

Step 10   Present the case to the hearing officer at the district-level conference.

Step 11   Appear before the school committee regarding the case.

Step 12   The teacher may appeal to have an arbitrator hear the case to make a binding decision about his or her employment in the school district. The grievance process may take one or more years to resolve. The teacher can also appeal to the judiciary system.

You will spend long hours at school and at home, including nights and weekends, working on the teacher dismissal process, which may extend into the next school year. To terminate an ineffective teacher, you must submit yourself to rigid discipline, hard work, industry, patience, and perseverance from the beginning to the end of the evaluation process.

3
Describing the Marginal and the Good Teacher

The marginal teacher lacks skills to ensure an efficient orderly classroom and safe learning environment for students.

To accurately and specifically describe a teacher's skills and behaviors during the evaluation process, you must completely understand the characteristics of a marginal teacher versus a good teacher. A marginal teacher's skill level falls between competent and incompetent. Moreover, a marginal teacher will put forth enough effort to get through a yearly evaluation process but reverts to a chronic poor teaching pattern shortly thereafter. Marginal teachers are unprepared, deficient in teaching skills, unable or unwilling to improve their teaching, have classroom management problems, display poor judgment, have a negative attitude about the teaching profession, and have a high tardiness and absence rate. A marginal teacher's problems may be the result of inadequate training or simply a negative attitude, or some combination that interferes with productive and effective classroom teaching performance. Figure 3.1 is a checklist consisting of six categories and more than forty questions that you can use at the beginning of the school year to determine if a marginal teacher is on your teaching staff. You will be able to quickly assess your teachers by answering the following questions.

Classroom Preparation, Planning, and Instruction	Yes	No
Does the teacher . . .		
1. Follow the scope and sequence of adopted curriculum?		
2. Prepare complete lesson plans?		
3. Use a variety of instructional time?		
4. Have adequate instructional strategies?		

Teaching	Yes	No
Does the teacher . . .		
1. Sit behind the desk while teaching?		
2. Have a range of instructional strategies?		
3. Summarize the lesson?		
4. Give students feedback?		
5. Teach interesting lessons?		
6. Use worksheets excessively?		
7. Involve students in classroom activities?		
8. Give clear and concise directions to students?		

School Procedures	Yes	No
Does the teacher . . .		
1. Maintain a phone log to contact parents?		
2. Maintain weekly grading sheets?		
3. E-mail parents and return e-mail replies?		
4. Check voicemail and return parent calls?		
5. Post a daily schedule of events?		
6. Have a system to take daily attendance?		
7. Assign students detention without notifying parents?		

Figure 3.1 Marginal Teacher Checklist

Classroom Management	Yes	No
Does the teacher . . .		
1. Have classroom management skills?		
2. Have classroom rules posted in the room?		
3. Have classroom procedures and routines?		
4. Monitor the entire class?		
5. Provide a safe learning environment?		
6. Maintain classroom decorum for learning to occur?		
7. Have a disproportionate number of student discipline referrals to office?		
8. Have trouble managing student misbehavior?		
9. Consistently handle misbehaviors?		
10. Receive many complaints from students and parents?		

Professional Responsibilities	Yes	No
Does the teacher . . .		
1. Arrive to work on time?		
2. Have excessive absences?		
2. Arrive on time for staff, department, and committee meetings?		
3. Participate in open houses and parent-teacher conferences?		
4. Participate in staff development activities?		

Relationship to Principal	Yes	No
Does the teacher . . .		
1. Consume too much of your administrative time?		
2. Display a negative attitude toward teaching?		
3. Seem uncooperative with other staff members?		
4. Have a negative attitude and refuse to do what is expected?		
5. Follow the suggestions to improve teaching performance?		
6. Appear resistant to changing teaching strategies?		
7. Postpone meetings with parents and students?		

Figure 3.1 Marginal Teacher Checklist (continued)

If the majority of your answers about the marginal teacher are "yes," you have an ineffective individual on your teaching staff. Unfortunately, many of these teachers are rated "highly qualified" in view of the fact that they have earned a bachelor's degree, hold an advanced degree in the subject they teach, and have met state certification and federal standards. In addition, many of these teachers appear highly qualified on paper, but in reality they are ineffective at managing and teaching children. As the principal, you must first help ineffective teachers improve their teaching performance, and if they fail to improve, you must take action to terminate ineffective teachers from the school district.

An effective teacher, however, manages a safe, orderly, and nurturing student learning environment. In the classroom of a high performing teacher, students are learning and the teacher comes to work on time, performs assigned duties, attends staff meetings, and follows school procedures. Good teachers exhibit a positive attitude and a strong commitment to the learning process. They use enthusiasm, expertise, and a wide range of teaching strategies and techniques to effectively teach their students. Figure 3.2 is an A through Z listing of good teacher indicators—consider these as the standards for the teachers on your staff.

In the following chapters, you will learn how to compile "airtight" documentation to prove beyond any lingering doubt that a marginal teacher is unsatisfactory and should be terminated from the school district.

A fighter for kids	*G*ood heart	*P*eaceful
*A*ccessible	*G*ood parental relationships	*P*ersonally passionate
*A*ctive listener	*G*ood procedures	*P*ersevering
*A*ffectionate to students	*G*reat lesson plans	*P*uts kids first
*A*ppreciates diversity	*H*appy	*R*esourceful
*C*aring	*H*as an outside life	*R*espects the parents
*C*harismatic	*H*onest	*S*afe environment
*C*ompassionate	*H*umorous	*S*ensitive
*C*oncerned	*I*nspires student self-confidence	*S*ense of efficacy
*C*ommitted to kids	*I*maginative	*S*elf-control
*C*ommunicates with parents	*I*s not perfect	*S*miles at kids
*C*reative	*J*oy of teaching	*S*ubject matter knowledge
*C*urious	*K*ids love them	*T*actful
*D*edicated to teaching	*K*nowledgeable	*T*eaches by example
*D*own-to-earth	*L*ifelong learner	*T*echnologically advanced
*E*nergetic	*L*oves kids	*T*rusting
*E*nthusiastic	*L*oves teaching	*U*nderstanding
*E*ven-tempered	*L*oyal	*U*nselfish attitude
*E*xcited about learning	*M*otivates students	*W*ell-managed classrooms
*E*xpects student success	*O*pen to new ideas	*W*illingness to change
*F*aithful	*O*rganized	
*F*lexible	*P*atient	
*G*entle		
*G*ood communicator		

Figure 3.2 Indicators of the Good Teacher

4 Starting the New School Year

Put forth extra effort at the beginning of the school year—and establish an evaluation policy—to have a successful school opening.

Get the school year off to a smooth start with your teaching staff by conducting a productive and informative first staff meeting, establishing detailed evaluation procedures, and setting clear procedures for administrative tasks and duties. Take this opportunity to set the stage for new teachers by setting clear standards and expectations for performance. Send a welcome letter in early August to all staff members conveying how glad you are to have them on your staff. Close the letter with a positive note about your expectation for a great upcoming school year. In your letters to all new teachers, assign them a mentor (coach) teacher, and include the mentor's name, grade level, subject area, and room number. Further, explain in your letter that the mentor teacher will give the new teacher someone to talk to about school procedures, instructional strategies, classroom management, and "what if" situations for a period of two years.

Holding an organized new teacher meeting is a great opportunity for you to help new teachers become familiar with you and each other and to provide important information and resources critical to succeeding in the classroom. Conduct a school building tour, introduce new teachers to their mentor teacher (coach) and support staff, and give them grade-level instructional resources. These tools include:

- The school building rules
- A list of types of student misbehaviors and management strategies
- School and classroom procedures
- Sample communication pieces to parents/guardians
- Suggestions for conducting parental conferences
- Detailed plans and procedures for the first two days of school
- Instructions on using student monitors
- Instructions on preparing a substitute teacher handbook
- A "Beginning-of-the-Year Survival Kit" for new teachers made up of pencils, paper, pens, Band-Aids, tissue, safety pins, a whistle, and other supplies.

As staff members enter the school building for the first staff meeting, welcome them with a banner that reads: *Welcome! This will be the best school year ever for XYZ School!* Start your meeting with an introduction of new staff members and discuss your expectations, school procedures, plans for the first days of school, and the teacher evaluation process. Give teachers individual copies of an up-to-date and comprehensive staff handbook and have teachers sign a form indicating that they received the handbook.

Following is a list of other important items you should discuss with your staff to get the school year off to an excellent start:

- **School Decision-Making Model:** Explain the school's bottom-to-top decision-making model where all staff members work together to identify problems and use their ideas to solve them. The decision-making model will allow staff members to influence issues that affect them while preserving your time and energy for resolving school problems.
- **Opening School Procedures:** Discuss school procedures for recording attendance, conducting fire drills, tornado drills, and shelter-in-place drills, maintaining and accessing health records, taking lunch counts, monitoring student lockers, and grading.
- **Master School Calendar:** Give each staff member a school year master calendar listing upcoming activities and events.
- **Weekly Bulletins:** Discuss the weekly staff bulletin issued before the start of each new week via either e-mail or a hard copy.
- **First Day of School:** Rehearse plans for the first day, including the time schedule, attendance, lunch count, hall supervision, bus arrival and departure procedures, and school dismissal.
- **September Open House:** Involve your staff members in planning the date and time for a September open house (Thursday is generally a good day of the week to hold the event).
- **School Engineer Message:** Invite the school engineer to discuss issues related to clocks, bells, fire extinguishers, fire alarms, damage to doors, windows, shades, tables, and other maintenance concerns. Ask the engineer to specifically discuss the procedure for reporting problems and how to make sure repairs occur as soon as possible.

You must build a productive and positive relationship with your staff to get the school year off to a good start. Focus on reducing the amount of teacher paperwork and limiting the length of staff meetings to give teachers more time to work in their classroom. Consider implementing the suggestions below to put forth an extra effort to get your new school year off to a great start.

Actions for the First Weeks of the School Year

- Set up a continental breakfast—beverage and muffins, rolls, or coffee cake— for your team.
- Plan a potluck lunch for all staff members—include teacher assistants, secretaries, food service staff, and custodial staff members.
- Ask teachers to introduce themselves, share what grade level and subject they teach, and give a brief statement about what they did during the summer.
- Emphasize that the school district's goal is to make student achievement the number one priority.
- Stress the educational philosophy of the school and explain the importance of setting high expectations for teachers and students.
- Discuss general school procedures—classroom management, lesson planning, and maintenance of records, duty schedules, procedures, routines, and student jobs/monitors.
- Encourage all teachers to have bulletin boards in place no later than the first week of school.
- Discuss school district discipline rules, school rules, classroom rules, classroom procedures, and communication with parents by letter, flyer, e-mail, and phone call.

Sample Resource Document 4.1
Letter Welcoming Staff
(Place on school letterhead)

Date

Dear Staff:

I hope you are having a restful and pleasant summer vacation. As the summer rapidly closes, the 20XX–20XX school year will present new challenges to all of us—new students, new staff members, new textbooks, a new state exam, and a new technology center.

This school year, we must rededicate ourselves to helping our students to reach their greatest academic potential. As always, we will work as a team to make our school the best in the XYZ School District. ABC Elementary School is the best-kept secret in the district. We are second to no other school in the district.

I am very enthusiastic about working with you to meet the challenge of educating our most precious resource, our children. Enclosed is the agenda for our first team meeting.

Again, welcome back! This will be the best year ever at ABC Elementary School.

Sincerely,

Principal

Enclosures

Sample Resource Document 4.2
Letter Assigning a Mentor Teacher to
Each New and Transferred Teacher
(Place on school letterhead)

Date

Name of Teacher

Address

Dear _____:

Welcome to _____ School. I want you to have a pro-
fessionally rewarding and educationally successful school year. I have assigned
_____ in room _____ to serve as your mentor teacher for this school
year. Your mentor teacher will help you with school policies and procedures and
provide encouragement and support as you create educational opportunities for
your students. In addition, I can assist you in any way possible to make this a
successful school year.

Again, welcome to _____ School. I am happy to
have you join our staff and I look forward to observing your enthusiasm and skill
in the classroom. This will be the best year ever for our staff, students, and
parents.

Sincerely,

Principal

cc: Mentor Teacher
    Enclosures
    Organizational Day Agenda

Sample Resource Document 4.3
School Decision-Making Model

Staff Members Compose the School Decision-Making Group

Phase 1
Establish standing committee

Phase 2
Committee meets

Phase 3
Committee develops
an action plan

Phase 4
Committee reports to the
decision-making body

Phase 5
- Recommendations
- Implement the plan
- Return to committee
- Revise plan

Phase 6
Plan implemented

Phase 7
Plan monitored by committee

Phase 8
Plan evaluated

Standing committee discusses the
following issues
during planning meetings.

Parental Involvement	School Climate	Staff Development	Student Rules	Curriculum & Instruction
Conference days Open house Parental visitations Classroom visits New student orientation Community relations	Safe school climate School atmosphere Transportation Honor roll students Auditorium programs	Staff workshops Support staff Student/teacher relationship Social activities	School rules Classroom rules Procedures Consequences Positive approaches	Explore new instructional strategies—books, computer programs—to improve student achievement

5

Organizing the Unsatisfactory Teacher Evaluation Binder

The most powerful asset to you during a campaign to dismiss an ineffective teacher is unsatisfactory teacher evaluation documentation, which can be easily organized into a binder (see the sample binder in Resource D: Sample Unsatisfactory Teacher Evaluation Documentation). This chapter focuses on organizing a three-ring binder to hold key communication pieces and your meticulous and systematic documentation of the teacher's performance. In addition to the documentation related to the specific teacher, the binder should contain various written materials that you have distributed to your staff members that clearly state school rules, policies, and teacher performance expectations. There should be few, if any, items in the binder that the teacher has not seen before or has not been able to access from various school sources—staff handbook, online school procedures, weekly bulletins, and so forth. At the dismissal meeting, the teacher should not be unfamiliar or surprised to see any of the documentation in the binder. It is essential to start assembling this binder at the beginning of the school year, because procrastination may result in insufficient documentation to support the termination of a teacher. A few sheets of paper or one formal observation will not meet the just cause requirements to terminate a teacher. The binder is organized in this manner to clearly demonstrate to an impartial hearing officer that you more than adequately supported and monitored the ineffective teacher. The Unsatisfactory Teacher Evaluation Binder should have a cover page, a table of contents, and tabs for sections I through XI. This binder will demonstrate beyond any lingering doubt that the teacher should be terminated from the school district.

The sections in the Unsatisfactory Teacher Evaluation Binder are as follows:

Section I	***The Beginning of the School Year*** This section includes the documentation you used to open the school year: staff welcome letters, details of your new teacher orientation, how you matched mentor (coach) teachers to new teachers, and your staff organization meeting agenda.
Section II	***Evaluation Process Made Known to All Teachers*** This section includes the types of communication between you and your staff that detailed how you would conduct teacher evaluations. Enclose a copy of the memorandum explaining the teacher evaluation process and a copy of the evaluation forms. Also include a copy of the letter identifying the teacher's evaluator and the roster with his or her signature verifying that he or she received the information.
Section III	***The Evaluation Process Applied to All Teachers*** This section provides an outline of the monthly monitoring forms and how they are used to document observations of all teachers.
Section IV	***Memoranda of Concerns/Memorandum of Accomplishment*** This section provides a copy of the letters or memoranda of concerns and the memorandum of accomplishments.
Section V	***Teacher Assistance*** This section contains the written letters that specify the instructional support that was provided to the teacher: staff handbook, lesson plan format outlining key instructional behaviors, school procedures, and procedures to refer students for disciplinary action.
Section VI	***Letters/Documents Relative to Assistance Provided*** This section contains a letter summarizing all the support given to the teacher.
Section VII	***Discipline Referrals*** This section includes a sample of the number of students the teacher sent to the principal for disciplinary support. It records the pending suspensions, actual suspensions, letters sent to parents, and other disciplinary actions requested by the teacher. Also include a summary report to show the date, time, reason, teacher's comments, teacher's recommendation, and administrative disposition for each referral. Also add all notes the teacher has written regarding classroom discipline problems, circling any misspelled words or grammatical errors in red ink.

Section VIII

Parental Complaints

This section contains the information to handle parental complaints—verbal or written—about the teacher. A copy of the parental complaint, which should include your comments and action taken, and a copy of the teacher's response are also placed in the Unsatisfactory Teacher Evaluation Binder. Use the misconduct provision in the master contract for serious parental complaints against a teacher related to sexual activities, drugs, and use of profane language, corporal punishment or verbal student abuse. These types of situations require you to work with central administration to immediately suspend the teacher with pay from all teaching duties to conduct an investigation into the complaint. Add the misconduct under the parental complaint section in the Unsatisfactory Teacher Evaluation Binder. A cautionary note: Do not mix up the misconduct and evaluation provisions in the master contract.

Section IX

Work Samples

This section is the collection of work samples from the teacher. Circle in red ink any misspelled words or grammatical errors to highlight the poor quality of work. Also compare work samples with the district and state standards to make sure the teacher is following the required curriculum. Add a copy of the district standards if the teacher is not meeting them.

Section X

Unsatisfactory Evaluation Letters and Evaluation

This section contains a sample of an unsatisfactory letter and the evaluation form issued to the teacher.

Section XI

Failure to Achieve a Satisfactory Step of Performance

This section contains a letter of intent to issue an unsatisfactory evaluation, a letter to schedule a conference, and the unsatisfactory evaluation form.

Binder Organization Tips

- *Prepare a cover page and a table of contents.*
- *Remember that the 11 sections in the binder describe the various types of evidence that will be needed to prove the unsatisfactory teacher evaluation.*
- *Put a tab on each section in the binder.*
- *Include all discipline referrals and other classroom management problems.*
- *Add any parental complaints regarding the teacher.*
- *Include copies of student work samples.*
- *Be sure that the completed Unsatisfactory Teacher Evaluation Binder is an impeccable professional document.*

You will add documentation throughout the evaluation process into each section of the Unsatisfactory Teacher Evaluation Binder. Also, before the school-level unsatisfactory performance meeting, make one copy of the binder for the teacher, one copy for the teacher's representative, and copies for future conferences and hearings. Most important, at the start of the teacher dismissal process, find out historical information about the teacher's background in the district file to make sure that the teacher is certified in the teaching subject area. If you issue an unsatisfactory evaluation to a teacher who is teaching outside of his or her certification area, the case may be overturned during the dismissal process.

**Sample Resource Document 5.1
Cover Page for the Unsatisfactory
Teacher Evaluation Documentation**
(Place on school letterhead)

Unsatisfactory Teacher Evaluation Documentation

for

_____

Submitted by _____, Principal

_____ School

_____, 20XX

Sample Resource Document 5.2
Skeleton Table of Contents for the
Unsatisfactory Teacher Evaluation Documentation

Sample Resource Document 5.3
Checklist/Collecting Historical Information
About the Teacher

_____ School

_____, 20XX–20XX

Teacher: _____

- Contact the Human Resources Department to verify the teacher's area of certification.

- Check the teacher's personnel file and read any previous letters warning the teacher about unsatisfactory teaching performance. Note the dates and the name(s) of the principal(s).

- Check the teacher's personnel file and read previous teacher evaluation documents. Carefully read for written comments about unsatisfactory teaching performance or warnings given by previous principals as well as comments providing suggestions for improvement. Note the dates and the name(s) of the principal(s).

- Check the local school file for any written warnings about an unsatisfactory teacher evaluation. Note the dates and the name(s) of the principal(s).

- Check the local school records to find out the number of days the teacher has been absent and the number of times the teacher has been late to work in relation to an unsatisfactory teacher evaluation.

- Contact the Human Resources Department to find out the number of days the teacher has been absent during the past three years.

- Check the local school file for any misconduct charges against the teacher in relation to an unsatisfactory teacher evaluation.

- Contact the department responsible for workers' compensation to determine if the teacher has filed claims for workers' compensation in relation to an unsatisfactory teacher evaluation.

Sample Resource Document 5.4
Summary of Monthly Formal and
Informal Classroom Observations

_____, 20XX

Principal: _____

Insert the names of all teachers in the first column, and add the dates in the section on the top column. Place the code in the grid to indicate the type of observation conducted.

Table key: WT: Walk Through
             IE: Informal Evaluation
             FE: Formal Evaluation

Teachers														

Sample Resource Document 5.5
Parental Complaint Letter
(Place on school letterhead)

Date

Name of Teacher

School Address

Dear _____:

Part _____, Section _____ of the _____ School District Contract states that when parental or public complaints are filed, the teacher must be made aware of the complaint. Therefore, I am forwarding the enclosed letter/ parental complaint form received about you on _____, 20XX.

Please plan to meet in my office on _____, 20XX at _____ p.m., to discuss this parental complaint. If this time is inconvenient, please contact my secretary to reschedule the meeting. We must resolve this complaint as soon as possible.

Sincerely,

Principal

Enclosure

Sample Resource Document 5.6
Parental Complaint Form

Date _____ Time _____ a.m./p.m.

Student _____ Grade _____ ID Number _____

Address _____

Person Filing Complaint _____

Relationship to Student _____

Phone Number: Home _____ Other _____ E-mail _____

Nature of Compliant _____

_____

_____

Action Requested _____

_____

Has a Previous Complaint Been Filed? Yes _____ No _____ Dates _____

Person(s) Spoken With: _____

_____
Name/Title/Department

_____
Name/Title/Department

Resolution _____

_____

_____

_____

Complaint Resolved _____ Further Action Necessary _____

_____
Signature/Title/Department

Sample Resource Document 5.7
Summary of Student Discipline Referrals

The following student discipline referrals were prepared by _____ to resolve a classroom problem:

Date	Time	Reasons

Note: Use a database program to sort student discipline referrals by date and time.

6

Observing All Teachers

Identify the marginal teacher early in the school year to provide support and allow a reasonable length of time for improvement.

A consistent comprehensive observation and appraisal process benefits all of the teachers on your staff. This is a critical component of your leadership responsibilities and most effective when clearly established and communicated at the start of the school year. You must be certain to observe teachers in accordance with state statutes, school district policies, and the master contract. This chapter highlights the preobservation meeting, classroom observation resources, a checklist observation form, teacher observations, feedback meeting, and providing support to the teacher. First, write a memorandum in early September to all teachers on your staff to explain the evaluation procedures and attach a copy of the observation forms. Second, write all teachers a letter identifying their evaluators by name and title and be sure that teachers initial a roster to identify receipt of the letter within the contractual limits. Do not place this important letter in the teacher's school mailbox—later on, you will not be able to successfully defend accusations from teachers that you failed to properly notify them of assigned evaluators. An impartial hearing officer will not uphold an unsatisfactory evaluation if it is proven that the principal failed to inform teachers of their evaluators.

You should use a variety of tools to record teacher observations, such as monthly monitoring forms to record informal and formal observations. In actuality, these forms are intended for an impartial hearing officer to see that all teachers were observed and no one was singled out. As you begin to conduct classroom observations, you will easily identify any disorderly classrooms. Find out what is happening in all classrooms, what teachers are doing or should be doing to help students, what students are learning, what the learning outcomes are, and what instructional strategies the teacher is using. You must resist temptation to let insignificant responsibilities prevent you from conducting morning and afternoon (announced or unannounced) teacher observations. Work in collaboration with your assistant principal, dean, or central administration staff to conduct teacher observations early in the school year—with you as the primary evaluator.

The Preobservation Meeting With the Teacher

Endeavor to build a trusting relationship with teachers to alleviate their discomfort related to your classroom observations. Arrange a time to meet with teachers to let them explain the lesson plan they plan to teach on the day of the observation. This premeeting should take about 15 to 25 minutes and give you the opportunity to become familiar with the lesson plan objective, introduction, body, and culminating activity. You should also ask teachers how they plan to use an attention-getting signal to alert students, state the lesson objective in the introduction, give students clear directions, check for understanding, provide student feedback, praise behavior, emphasize rules and procedures, and summarize the lesson. Ask teachers about any unusual group or individual circumstances before observing the lesson. Stress to the teachers that you will focus on practices to help them improve. At this meeting, schedule a feedback meeting within the next three to five school days following the observation. You will not need to schedule any future teacher preobservation meetings because all other observations are unannounced.

Teacher Observation Resources

Use preobservation meetings to inform teachers about the methods you will use to collect evaluation information about their teaching. See page 37 for a brief overview of the various observation resources that you may use to evaluate teachers in a specific, productive, and comprehensive manner.

Each of the earlier mentioned observation resources/techniques has its advantages and disadvantages, and you must consider your own preferences and feedback from your teachers to decide which one to use. Remember to use your school district's required observation forms and an evaluation instrument to evaluate teachers.

Avoid Only Using a Checklist

You cannot use only a checklist to collect objective evidence to compile documentation to make a recommendation to terminate a teacher. A checklist is merely a list of vague terms for you to record evidence during a 5- to 15-minute *informal* observation or walk-through observation. You should conduct informal observations for every teacher at least twice per day (morning and afternoon) to

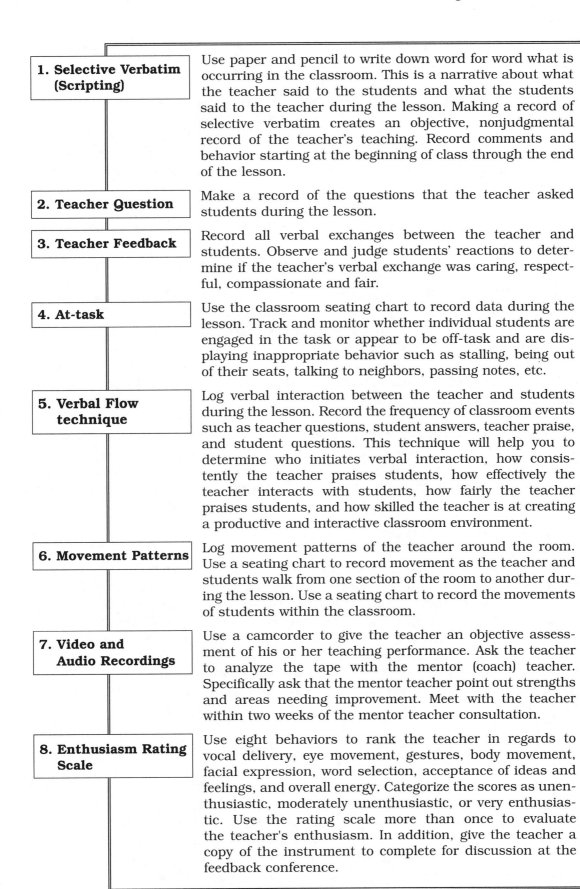

1. Selective Verbatim (Scripting)	Use paper and pencil to write down word for word what is occurring in the classroom. This is a narrative about what the teacher said to the students and what the students said to the teacher during the lesson. Making a record of selective verbatim creates an objective, nonjudgmental record of the teacher's teaching. Record comments and behavior starting at the beginning of class through the end of the lesson.
2. Teacher Question	Make a record of the questions that the teacher asked students during the lesson.
3. Teacher Feedback	Record all verbal exchanges between the teacher and students. Observe and judge students' reactions to determine if the teacher's verbal exchange was caring, respectful, compassionate and fair.
4. At-task	Use the classroom seating chart to record data during the lesson. Track and monitor whether individual students are engaged in the task or appear to be off-task and are displaying inappropriate behavior such as stalling, being out of their seats, talking to neighbors, passing notes, etc.
5. Verbal Flow technique	Log verbal interaction between the teacher and students during the lesson. Record the frequency of classroom events such as teacher questions, student answers, teacher praise, and student questions. This technique will help you to determine who initiates verbal interaction, how consistently the teacher praises students, how effectively the teacher interacts with students, how fairly the teacher praises students, and how skilled the teacher is at creating a productive and interactive classroom environment.
6. Movement Patterns	Log movement patterns of the teacher around the room. Use a seating chart to record movement as the teacher and students walk from one section of the room to another during the lesson. Use a seating chart to record the movements of students within the classroom.
7. Video and Audio Recordings	Use a camcorder to give the teacher an objective assessment of his or her teaching performance. Ask the teacher to analyze the tape with the mentor (coach) teacher. Specifically ask that the mentor teacher point out strengths and areas needing improvement. Meet with the teacher within two weeks of the mentor teacher consultation.
8. Enthusiasm Rating Scale	Use eight behaviors to rank the teacher in regards to vocal delivery, eye movement, gestures, body movement, facial expression, word selection, acceptance of ideas and feelings, and overall energy. Categorize the scores as unenthusiastic, moderately unenthusiastic, or very enthusiastic. Use the rating scale more than once to evaluate the teacher's enthusiasm. In addition, give the teacher a copy of the instrument to complete for discussion at the feedback conference.

support the formal evaluation. Downey, Steffy, English, Frase, and Poston (2004, p. 21) endorse the following five-step, walk-through observation structure:

Step 1: Student Orientation to the Work—Do students appear to be attending to the lesson or assignment when you first walk into the room?

Step 2: Curricular Decision Points—What objective(s) has the teacher chosen to teach at this time and how aligned are they to the prescribed district or state written curriculum?

Step 3: Instructional Decision Points—What instructional practices are being chosen by the teacher to use at this time to help students learn the curriculum objectives?

Step 4: "Walk-the-Wall" Curricular and Instructional Decisions—What evidence is there of past objectives taught and/or instructional decisions used to teach the objectives that are present in the classroom—walk-the-walls, portfolios, and projects in the room?

Step 5: Safety and Health Issues—Are there any noticeable safety or health issues that need to be addressed?

These five steps will enable you to gather evidence about the teacher's teaching. Moreover, you should use these steps to strengthen the formal teacher evaluation form. Once again, you must use the informal observation form in concert with your school district's formal observation instrument to terminate a teacher.

Formal Teacher Observations

The formal observation is important to gather evidence to prove that the teacher should be terminated from the school district. On the day of the teacher observation, you should begin recording at the start of the lesson for approximately 45 minutes or until the end of the class period. You will need a table in the back of the classroom to set up the evaluation materials, including a copy of the lesson plan, seating chart, and an observation form to record what is occurring in the classroom. Collect worksheet samples and examine the quality and quantity of busywork (e.g., photocopies) to ensure that the subject areas meet district standards.

The Feedback Meeting With the Teacher

You will need to conduct a private feedback meeting with the teacher to gather more information about the lesson you observed. This meeting should last between 30 and 45 minutes. Make sure that you come across to teachers as self-confident, controlled, and interested in helping them improve teaching performance. Begin the feedback meeting with positive statements that state specifically what you think the teacher did well during the lesson. You may wish to further your evaluation by asking teachers hypothetical questions about what they would have done if certain scenarios occurred in the classroom during a lesson. It is important that you be a good listener and allow time for teachers to talk—but you may paraphrase what teachers say for clarification and prompt them to come up with ideas to improve their teaching performance. Continue to ask teachers questions about what worked well and why it was effective, and what aspect of the lesson they disliked and why it was not successful. Next, describe the narrative you recorded during the observation without judgment by factually reporting what the teachers said to students and what the students said to them. You must be specific regarding what you observed by using facts and evidence collected during the observation. At the end of the meeting, review the points you want the teacher to remember about successful teaching, placing emphasis on your recommended teaching improvements. Always end conferences by asking teachers how they can help improve their own teaching performance. If you think that a teacher's teaching performance may advance to the unsatisfactory evaluation level, you should ask your assistant principal to attend the meeting to take note. Also, you should advise teachers that they may bring a representative of their association or a legal or other type of advocate to the meeting to ensure that their due process rights are not violated.

Communicating to Teachers

Written communication is proof that you adequately informed teachers of their ineffective classroom teaching. For that reason, you must write a memorandum or letter of concern to offer the teacher specific improvement suggestions. You may use the following key descriptors within a memorandum or letter of concern sent to the teacher:

• Failed to be . . .	• Was inconsistent
• Failed to communicate . . .	• Was not authorized to . . .
• Failed to produce . . .	• Was not always prepared
• Failed to improve . . .	• Did not monitor . . .
• Failed to implement . . .	• Did not have . . .
• Failed to follow suggestions	• Does not participate
• Failed to accept suggestions	• Did not exhibit . . .
• Failed to maintain . . .	• Displayed negative . . .
• Failed to have . . .	• Consistently failed to . . .
• Failed to follow guidelines	• Has made no substantial improvement
• Failed to provide sufficient . . .	• Proceeded without proper . . .

About three weeks after giving the teacher your memorandum or letter of concern, you should conduct another observation based upon the letter or memorandum of concern to assess if the teacher made the improvements as recommended. If the teacher accomplished the teaching improvements, note it in the letter or memorandum, but still emphasize other improvement suggestions. This letter or memorandum proves that the teacher was informed about his or her teaching problems and that you provided improvement suggestions. This critical documentation assists you in proving beyond any shadow of lingering doubt that the teacher is unsatisfactory and should be terminated from the school district. Copies of the letters or memoranda of concern or memorandum of accomplishments are placed in the Unsatisfactory Teacher Evaluation Binder.

At the next feedback meeting, ask the teacher to report on the progress made since the last observation. Send the second memorandum of concern to the teacher specifying the areas of improvement required to reach a satisfactory teaching level. You must continue to make unannounced observations to determine if the teacher is making progress to improve teaching performance. Throughout the dismissal process, you must follow up each meeting with a letter or memorandum of concern and accomplishments.

Thirty Sample Resources

The resources in this chapter have 30 samples to develop compelling and powerful evidence to substantiate the unsatisfactory teacher evaluation. You may use some of the resource letters to provide the teacher with support and assistance. These short letters are specifically designed for an impartial hearing officer to quickly read about the support and assistance given to the teacher. An impartial hearing officer does not have time to read long rambling letters with spelling or grammatical errors. To make it easier for the hearing officer to follow your documentation, write short letters and avoid using educational jargon—IEP, SSR, ESL, LEP, Time-out, Reflection room, or Accommodation room. Furthermore, you should be on the safe side by having another evaluator proofread your written communication to avoid harsh criticism and lessened credibility during the dismissal hearings. You must place copies of all memos and letters into the Unsatisfactory Teacher Evaluation Binder.

Sample Resource Document 6.1
Letter Identifying the Teacher's Evaluator

Date

Name of Teacher

School Address

Dear _____:

Teacher evaluation is a valuable tool used to improve classroom teaching performance and promote professional growth. This is consistent with the contract between the _____ school district and the *(name of the bargaining unit)* and state statutes section 9.14. The evaluation procedures for this school year will ensure that a teacher's strengths as well as weaknesses are discussed to enhance professional development to improve student achievement.

Part _____, Section _____ of the _____contract states that the identification of the evaluator must be made known to the teacher by name and title by the third Friday at the beginning of the school year. I shall conduct your performance evaluation during the 20XX–20XX school year, with collaboration with other administrative and supervisory staff assigned to _____
School. In the event that someone else must serve in my capacity, that person will conduct your evaluation.

Sincerely,

Principal

Sample Resource Document 6.2
Receipt of Letter Identifying the Evaluator
(Place on school letterhead)

_____ School

Staff Roster for Friday, September 25, 20XX

Room Number	Teacher Name	Teacher Signature
1		
2		
3		
4		
5		
6		
7		
8		
9		
10		
11		
12		
13		
14		
15		
16		
17		
18		
19		
20		
21		

Sample Resource Document 6.3
Memorandum Explaining the Evaluation Process
(Place on school letterhead)

Date:

To:

From:

Re:

The purpose of the evaluation process is to improve teaching performance and promote the teacher's professional growth. This memorandum explains procedures that will be used to evaluate teachers this school year: the informal observation, the formal observation, and the summative evaluation. Attached is a copy of each evaluation form.

Informal Observations/Evaluations

Teachers should expect informal observations of approximately 10 to 15 minutes in length throughout the school year. A copy of the informal evaluation form will be given to the teacher after the observation.

Formal Evaluations

The school district's formal evaluation form will be used to conduct teacher observations. A formal evaluation is scheduled for the entire class period; however, it may be divided into two short observations. Teachers are required to schedule a 15-minute preobservation meeting with me to discuss the lesson plan for the day of the observation. Teachers will receive a copy of the formal evaluation form to complete a self-assessment—an honest self-assessment of their teaching. Within three to five days following the formal observation, a postobservation conference will be held to discuss the teacher's strengths, weaknesses, and improvement suggestions.

Year-End Evaluation (Summative)

The summative evaluation conference is held during April or May to evaluate school year teaching performance. The district's evaluation form will be completed and sent to the Human Resources Department to be placed in the teacher's personnel file. If you have any questions, please see my secretary to schedule a meeting to discuss the evaluation procedures.

Attachments

Sample Resource Document 6.4
Informal Observation/Evaluation Form

_____ School

Teacher _____ Subject/Grade _____ Date _____

Time of day _____ Class period _____ Evaluation number _____

Total students assigned to class/in class _____/_____

Indicators	Satisfactory	Marginal	Needs Improvement	Unsatisfactory
1. Instructional skills				
2. Presentation clarity				
3. Responding to students				
4. Ending lesson				
5. Classroom management				
6. Positive learning climate				
7. Communication				

Comments_____

_____

_____

_____

If you want to discuss this evaluation checklist with me, please see my secretary to schedule an appointment.

Thank you,

Principal

Sample Resource Document 6.5
Letter Summarizing a Meeting Held With the Teacher
(Place on school letterhead)

Date

Name of Teacher

School Address

Dear _____:

This letter is a summary of the meeting held with me in my office on _____ at _____a.m./p.m.

At the beginning of the meeting, I stated my concerns about your inability to effectively manage and teach students in your classroom. My concerns were as follows:

    1.

    2.

    3.

We also discussed opportunities made available in the school district to help you improve your teaching performance. I also gave you the following recommendations to improve your teaching skills:

    1.

    2.

    3.

I want to continue supporting your efforts to improve your teaching performances, but the ultimate responsibility rests with you to improve your teaching effectiveness.

Sincerely,

Principal

Sample Resource Document 6.6
Letter Summarizing Second
Meeting Held With the Teacher
(Place on school letterhead)

Date

Name of Teacher

School Address

Dear _____:

This letter is a summary of the second meeting held with me in my office on _____ at _____a.m./p.m.

At the beginning of the meeting, I stated my concerns about your inability to effectively manage and teach students in your classroom. My concerns were as follows:

1.

2.

3.

We also discussed opportunities made available in the school district to help you improve your teaching performance. I also gave you the following recommendations to improve your teaching skills:

1.

2.

3.

I want to continue supporting your efforts to improve your teaching performances, but the ultimate responsibility rests with you to improve your teaching effectiveness.

Sincerely,

Principal

Sample Resource Document 6.7
Improvement Suggestions
for the Memorandum of Concerns

I. (Concern) Preparation for instruction

A. Recommendations *(be specific and concise)*
B. Follow the adopted school district reading curriculum
C. Lesson plan must be easy to read and follow
D. State lesson objective at the beginning of lesson
E. Have enough materials for all students

II. (Concern) Presentation of organized instruction

A. Gain the attention of students before starting the lesson
B. Do not stand in one spot too long
C. Do not take too long to start teaching students
D. Demonstrate more teaching energy
E. Connect with the students during the lesson
F. Talk and interact with the entire class, not just half of the class
G. Give clear and simple directions
H. Provide examples and illustrations
I. Rearrange physical environment for instruction
J. Summarize major points
K. Motivate students to get ready for a lesson
L. Smile while teaching and have fun teaching
M. Show more self-confidence teaching

III. (Concern) Assessment of student performance

A. Summarize the lesson
B. Provide positive feedback to students
C. Ask open-ended questions
D. Develop better transitions to the next lesson
E. Seek student feedback

IV. (Concern) Classroom management

A. Post your classroom rules to let students know them
B. Develop procedures to hand out materials
C. Develop procedures for student participation (raise your hand, not yelling out in class)
D. Develop procedures for moving from center rug to seats
E. Use student helpers
F. Do not wait too long to recognize students
G. Develop procedures for collecting and returning homework
H. Hold class discussions demonstrating how children should do their work
I. Unclasp your hands

J. Show focus and energy and be mobile in classroom—teach from all areas of the room

K. Monitor the entire class

L. Do not talk too long to one group of students—monitor the entire class

M. Avoid turning your back too long on students

N. Handwriting on whiteboard must follow the adopted district plan

O. Give verbal warnings to students and follow through

P. Do not use threats that cannot be acted upon

Q. Use students' names

R. Plan questions or write them out

S. Do not talk over student noise

T. Do not allow unacceptable behavior such as fighting in your classroom

U. Do not be influenced by being a popular teacher

V. (Concern) Positive learning climate

A. Give students more positive responses

B. Develop reward systems—activity, merchandise, recognition, and social rewards

C. Return graded homework

D. Develop motivational activities

VI. (Concern) Communication

A. Become a more assertive teacher

B. Improve your vocal delivery, eyes, gestures, and facial expression

C. Use a strong voice

D. Talk more slowly to students

E. Verbally and nonverbally respond to misbehaviors

F. Avoid using "Shhh"

G. Use polite language such as "thank you" and "please"

Note: The Memorandum of Concerns examples should be related to the school district teacher assessment indicators.

Sample Resource Document 6.8
Memorandum of Concerns No. 1
(Place on school letterhead)

Date:

To:

From:

Re: Concerns and Teaching Improvements Suggestions

This memorandum of concerns is written to make clear my concerns about your teaching performance and offers some improvement suggestions.

Concern 1: *(State concern and give an example)*

Recommendations: *(Be specific and concise)*

A.

B.

C.

D.

Concern 2: *(State concern and give an example)*

Recommendations: *(Be specific and concise)*

A.

B.

C.

D.

Concern 3: *(State concern and give an example)*

Recommendations: *(Be specific and concise)*

A.

B.

C.

D.

In closing, I want you to have a successful teaching experience, but you must improve your teaching performance. Clearly, it is up to you to improve. If you have any questions about this memorandum, you may put them in writing no later than _____, or you can see my secretary to schedule a meeting to discuss this memorandum of concerns.

Note: See suggestions list for the memorandum of concerns. Follow up the Memorandum of Concerns with a Memorandum of Accomplishments.

Sample Resource Document 6.9
Memorandum of Accomplishments
(Place on school letterhead)

Date:

To:

From:

Re: Accomplishment of Teaching Suggestions

A Memorandum of Concerns was sent to you on _____, 20XX listing my concerns about your teaching, and I gave you _____ suggestions to improve your classroom teaching. This Memorandum of Accomplishments is to determine if you accomplished these improvements within your teaching over the past ____ weeks. I have used the rating scale below to assess your teaching improvements.

    1. Unsatisfactory Accomplishment
    2. Marginal Accomplishment
    3. Satisfactory Accomplishment
    4. Above Average Accomplishment
    5. Excellent Accomplishment

Concern 1: Accomplishment of Suggestions

Recommendations:

Concern 2: Accomplishment of Suggestions

Recommendations:

Concern 3: Accomplishment of Suggestions

Recommendations:

Although you made a few teaching changes, your teaching performance, in my opinion, is still unsatisfactory. You must successfully implement the other teaching suggestions as specified in the first memorandum of concerns. I will continue to conduct informal and formal observations to evaluate your teaching performance. I want to be as clear as possible that if your teaching performance does not improve within the next 20 school days, you may receive an unsatisfactory teacher evaluation. If you have questions about this memorandum, you can write a letter no later than the next 10 school days or you can see my secretary to schedule a meeting with me to discuss the memorandum. At this meeting, you may be represented by anyone of your choice.

Note: The Memorandum of Concerns can list as many items as necessary to document the unsatisfactory teacher evaluation. The Memorandum of Accomplishments must include the concerns and recommendations you mentioned in the Memorandum of Concerns.

Sample Resource Document 6.10
Memorandum of Concerns No. 2
(Place on school letterhead)

Date:

To:

From:

Re: Concerns and Teaching Improvements Suggestions

This memorandum of concerns is written to make clear my concerns about your teaching performance and offers some improvement suggestions.

Concern 1: *(State concern and give an example)*

Recommendations: *(Be specific and concise)*

A.

B.

C.

D.

Concern 2: *(State concern and give an example)*

Recommendations: *(Be specific and concise)*

A.

B.

C.

D.

Concern 3: *(State concern and give an example)*

Recommendations: *(Be specific and concise)*

A.

B.

C.

D.

In closing, I want you to have a successful teaching experience, but you must improve your teaching performance. Clearly, it is up to you to improve. If you have any questions about this memorandum, you may put them in writing no later than _____, or you can see my secretary to schedule a meeting to discuss this memorandum of concerns.

Note: See improvement suggestions for the Memorandum of Concerns. Follow up the Memorandum of Concerns with a Memorandum of Accomplishments to assess whether or not the teacher made improvements.

Sample Resource Document 6.11
Peer Observation Form
(Place on school letterhead)

Date

Name of Teacher

School Address

Dear _____:

I would like you to visit _____ classroom to observe his/her classroom management procedures and instructional techniques for small and large
group instruction. Arrangements have been made for a substitute to teach your
class on_____, from 9:30 a.m. to 11:00 a.m.

During the observation, use the attached Peer Observation Form to learn
how _____ operates his/her classroom. Pay attention to his/her rules,
procedures, and routines, classroom seating arrangement, cooperative grouping
learning, teaching skills, and lesson closure and transitions between lessons.

Again, I stand ready to assist you in making this school year a successful
teaching experience. We will discuss the observation at our next meeting on
_____ at _____ p.m. in my office.

Sincerely,

Principal

Enclosure

Sample Resource Document 6.11a
Peer Observation Form

School _____ Date _____ Time _____ Class Period _____

Teacher Observing _____ Name of Teacher _____

I. Starting the School Day

1. How did the teacher escort the students to the classroom?
2. How did the teacher greet the students?
3. What communication took place between the teacher and the students?
4. What opening-the-school-day actions occurred in the classroom?
5. Were they planned or on-the-spot decisions? Did the actions seem like work or fun?
6. How did the teacher take attendance? (Using the seating chart? Homework turned in? Other system?)
7. How did the teacher collect money (lunch/supply/field trip)?

II. Classroom Instruction

1. Did the teacher begin the lesson with a motivational activity to capture the students' attention?
2. How did the teacher make the lesson objective known to students?
3. How did the teacher begin the lesson quickly?
4. What was the level of student participation?
5. How did the teacher keep the students motivated during the lesson?
6. How did the teacher use a variety of questions?
7. Did the teacher stand in one location or move around the room?
8. Did the teacher's position affect discipline problems?

III. Lesson Closure

1. How did the teacher close the lesson?
2. How was completed work collected?
3. How did the teacher assign homework?

IV. Classroom Management

1. What was included in the teacher's classroom management plan?
2. What classroom management strategies were used to handle minor misbehaviors?
3. What features reflected the teacher's enthusiasm (i.e., vocal delivery, eye movement, gestures, body movement, facial expression, word selection, acceptance of ideas and feelings, and overall energy)?
4. How did the teacher end the class?

V. Observation Conclusions

1. Did you find any strategies that could help you improve your teaching? Please explain them.

Sample Resource Document 6.12
Letter Reviewing Assistance Provided to the Teacher
(Place on school letterhead)

Date

Name of Teacher

School Address

Dear _____:

During the past _____ weeks, the following recommendations were made to help you improve your teaching performance:

-
-
-

I would like to meet with you to discuss these recommendations for teaching improvement and to discuss your progress. Please contact my secretary as soon as possible to schedule an appointment with me.

Sincerely,

Principal

Sample Resource Document 6.13
Letter—Teacher to Shadow a Teacher in Another School
(Place on school letterhead)

Date

Name of Teacher

School Address

Dear _____:

As we have discussed earlier, opportunities are available for teachers to observe classes and teachers in other schools in our district. I have arranged for you to spend a day at _____ School, which is located at _____.

You are to report to the school office to meet with Mrs. Beverly Martinez, Principal, on _____, at 8:00 a.m. You will spend the day observing in _____ fifth grade classroom. He is an experienced teacher who has excellent classroom management skills as well as instructional techniques. If you believe it would be worthwhile, I can arrange to have _____ visit your classroom, too.

Sincerely,

Principal

Sample Resource Document 6.14
Letter Confirming Arrangements for the Teacher
(Place on school letterhead)

Date

Name of Teacher

School Address

Dear _____:

Opportunities are available for teachers to observe classes at other schools in the district school. Per your request, arrangements have been made for you to visit _____ School, which is located at _____.
You are to report to the office to get a visitor's pass and then report to Mr./Mrs. _____ at ____ a.m. _____, 20XX. You will spend the morning session in the ___ grade classroom of _____, an experienced teacher.

If you feel that this is a valuable learning experience for you, the teacher can also visit your classroom. Again, I stand ready to assist you in making this school year a successful teaching experience.

Sincerely,

Principal

Sample Resource Document 6.15
Letter Referring the Teacher to
Specific Sections in the Teacher Handbook
(Place on school letterhead)

Date

Name of Teacher

School Address

Dear _____:

I am concerned that you may not understand some of the school procedures. You received a copy of the Teacher Handbook containing information about school procedures at the beginning of the school year. I am requesting that you familiarize yourself with the following school procedures in the staff handbook:

Handbook Section	**Procedures**	**Page Number**

You may discuss these procedures with your mentor teacher, other staff members, or feel free to discuss them with me.

Thank you,

Principal

Note: Include a copy of the pages cited in the staff handbook or the table of contents in the Unsatisfactory Teacher Evaluation Binder.

Sample Resource Document 6.16
Letter Identifying Articles on Classroom Management
(Place on school letterhead)

Date

Name of Teacher

School Address

Dear _____:

I made copies of three articles that may help you to improve your classroom management and teaching techniques. They are:

-
-
-

Sincerely,

Principal

Enclosures

Note: Include a copy of the article in the Unsatisfactory Teacher Evaluation Binder.

Sample Resource Document 6.17
Classroom Management Articles
(Place on school letterhead)

Date

Name of Teacher

School Address

Dear _____:

Enclosed you will find copies of the following articles, which should help you to improve your classroom management and teaching techniques:

1. "Proactive Teaching Strategies"
2. "Basic Classroom Management"
3. "The Good Teacher"
4. "A Teacher Making/Made the Difference"

As always, I stand ready to assist you in making this school year a successful teaching experience.

Sincerely,

Principal

Enclosures

Sample Resource Document 6.18
Staff Development Bulletin
(Place on school letterhead)

Date

Name of Teacher

School Address

Dear _____:

The _____ School District Staff Development Bulletin offers several workshops that would be beneficial to help you improve your classroom teaching performance. I would like to suggest that you enroll in the following class(es):

-
-
-

Registration forms are available in the school office, and the school will pay your tuition fees to attend these workshops.

As always, I stand ready to assist you in making this school year a successful teaching experience.

Sincerely,

Principal

Note: Include a copy of the workshop pages in the Unsatisfactory Teacher Evaluation Binder.

Sample Resource Document 6.19
Spring Staff Development Bulletin
(Place on school letterhead)

Date

Name of Teacher

School Address

Dear _____:

The XYZ School District Spring 20XX Staff Development Bulletin lists several inservice classes that would be beneficial to your classroom teaching performance. I suggest that you enroll in the following classes:

- Reading in the Content Areas
- Assertive Discipline
- Survival Skills for the Classroom Teacher

As always, I stand ready to assist you in making this a successful teaching experience. The head secretary in the school office has the registration forms.

Sincerely,

Principal

Sample Resource Document 6.20
Letter Encouraging the Teacher to Attend a Convention
(Place on school letterhead)

Date
Name of Teacher
School Address

Dear _____:

The _____ Teachers' Convention will be held from _____, 20XX to _____, 20XX at _____ *(specific location)*. I found several excellent workshops listed in the bulletin that may assist you to improve your teaching performance. I suggest that you attend the following workshops:

Title	Date	Time	Room

1.

2.

3.

Sincerely,

Principal

Note: Include a copy of the convention booklet in the Unsatisfactory Teacher Evaluation Binder.

Sample Resource Document 6.21
Letter Providing Videotapes on Classroom
Management/Instructional Strategies
(Place on school letterhead)

Date

Name of Teacher

School Address

Dear _____:

Your classroom management and teaching strategies are in need of improvement. Accordingly, I am providing you with a copy of the following CD/DVDs that illustrate classroom management techniques and instructional strategies. Once you view these CD/DVDs, I would like to meet with you next week to discuss how you may incorporate these practices into your classroom.

-
-
-

Please see my secretary to schedule a meeting as soon as possible.

Sincerely,

Principal

Enclosures

Sample Resource Document 6.22
Series of Videotapes on Classroom
Management/Instructional Strategies
(Place on school letterhead)

Date

Name of Teacher

School Address

Dear _____:

As a resource for classroom teachers, a series of videotapes was recently purchased by our school district, which features _____, who is one of the leading experts in the field of education for teacher survival techniques. I feel that this series offers excellent information that should help you to become a more effective teacher. Therefore, I suggest that you view them in the school library within the next week:

1. *The Effective Teacher* (30 minutes)

2. *Lesson Planning* (25 minutes)

3. *Effective Classroom Management* (30 minutes)

4. *Classroom Rules and Procedures* (28 minutes)

5. *Key Instructional Behaviors* (35 minutes)

At our next postobservation conference, we will discuss the new strategies that you gleaned from these videotapes.

I stand ready to assist you in making this a successful school year.

Sincerely,

Principal

Sample Resource Document 6.23
Videotapes on Teaching
(Place on school letterhead)

Date

Name of Teacher

School Address

Dear _____:

I am providing you with the following videotapes, which demonstrate successful classroom management techniques:

- *Increasing Student Achievement Through Cooperative Learning*
- *Creating an Atmosphere for Positive Student Interaction*

I want you to view these tapes and then meet with me to discuss how you might incorporate these techniques into your classroom. Please see my secretary to schedule a meeting with me.

Sincerely,

Principal

Enclosures

Sample Resource Document 6.24
Cooperative Learning Videotapes
(Place on school letterhead)

Date

Name of Teacher

School Address

Dear _____:

I am providing you the following videotapes, which demonstrate successful cooperative group learning techniques:

- *Structuring the Classroom Environment for Large Groups*
- *Small Group and Individualized Instruction*

I want you to view these tapes and then meet with me to discuss how you plan to incorporate these techniques into your classroom. Please see my secretary to schedule a meeting with me.

Sincerely,

Principal

Sample Resource Document 6.25
Letter Referring the Teacher to Internet Sites
(Place on school letterhead)

Date

Name of Teacher

School Address

Dear _____:

The new computer in your classroom is connected to the Internet. There are some excellent sites dealing with effective teaching strategies to help you to improve your teaching performance. I would like you to explore the following effective teaching strategies Web sites:

- www.teachhelp.com
- www.Desperateteacher.com
- www.effectiveteachers.com

I also listed these sites in the weekly staff bulletin. Our computer specialist can assist you in locating these excellent Web sites, if necessary. You may wish to print out some of these effective teaching strategies and begin incorporating them into your teaching.

Sincerely,

Principal

Enclosure

Sample Resource Document 6.26
Teacher Talk Internet Site
(Place on school letterhead)

Date

Name of Teacher

School Address

Dear _____:

I would like you to log on to the National Teacher Talk Web page, which is specifically designed for new classroom teachers to discuss and share classroom issues. The Web site address is http://www.teachertalk.com. This is an excellent site to obtain information about classroom instruction and classroom management. In addition, the site offers message pages where you can leave specific questions for other teachers to answer.

If you have any questions about accessing this Web site, please contact me.

Sincerely,

Principal

Sample Resource Document 6.27
Letter to Purchase Books
(Place on school letterhead)

Date

Name of Teacher

School Address

Dear _____:

Last year all classroom teachers received $70 from the school to purchase professional books. Attached is the 20XX–20XX _____ Publishing Company educational catalog that may have effective teaching books. If you would like to purchase some books, please complete the order form and give it to my secretary on or before October 31, 20XX.

Sincerely,

Principal

Attachment

Sample Resource Document 6.28
Letter Referring the Teacher to the Weekly Bulletin
(Place on school letterhead)

Date

Name of Teacher

School Address

Dear _____:

The weekly staff bulletin is disseminated each Thursday morning and is posted on the school Web page. The weekly bulletin has sections for student and teacher news and awards, daily activities, staff reminders, and future school activities. Some of the staff reminders include suggestions for picking up students on time and quietly escorting them to their classrooms.

I want you to reread the teacher reminder in future weekly bulletins to gain valuable and effective teaching tips. Thank you.

Sincerely,

Principal

Note: Include a copy of the weekly bulletins in the Unsatisfactory Teacher Evaluation Binder.

Sample Resource Document 6.29
Letter Requesting Classroom Procedures
(Place on school letterhead)

Date

Name of Teacher

School Address

Dear _____:

A successfully managed classroom has many procedures in place that are clearly communicated to students. I am concerned that after the fifth week of the school year, your students do not know your classroom rules and procedures. Please send to me a written record of your classroom procedures by _____, 20XX. Your response must include the following procedures:

A. Beginning Class

    1. Taking and recording attendance and tardiness
    2. Providing academic warm-ups
    3. Distributing materials
    4. Beginning the lesson
    5. Gaining students' attention

B. Classroom and School Areas

    1. Drinks, bathroom, pencil sharpener
    2. Student storage
    3. Learning centers
    4. Playground and school grounds

C. Work Requirements and Procedures

    1. Paper heading
    2. Use of pen or pencil
    3. Writing on the back of paper
    4. Neatness and legibility
    5. Incomplete work
    6. Late work
    7. Definition of "working alone"
    8. Passing out books and supplies
    9. Out-of-seat policies
    10. Talking among students (general and during seatwork)
    11. Conduct during interruptions
    12. Marking/grading papers

Sincerely,

Principal

Sample Resource Document 6.30
Focus on Teaching
(Place on school letterhead)

Date

Name of Teacher

School Address

Dear _____:

In order to improve your teaching skills, I suggest that you focus on making improvements in the specific performance areas listed below:

Classroom organization and procedures
Physical organization
Expectations
Grading system
Learning environment
Positive teacher-student interaction
Rewards and encouragement
Multicultural awareness
Lesson planning and presentation
Introduction
Motivation
Organization
Closure
Assessment
Instructional techniques
Cooperative learning
Reading instruction
Mathematics instruction
Student discipline
Conflict resolution
Assertive discipline

I want to meet with you to discuss these improvement suggestions and the progress you believe that you have made to improve your teaching. Please see my secretary to schedule an appointment to discuss this letter.

Sincerely,

Principal

7

Implementing an Intensive Assistance Plan

You must provide support and assistance to help the marginal teacher improve his or her teaching performance.

Implementing an intensive assistance plan requires your diligence in dutifully documenting actions as you endeavor to improve a teacher's teaching deficiencies. Your school district may require a specific intensive assistance plan. If your district does not require an intensive assistance plan, use the Memorandum of Concerns and Memorandum of Accomplishments (see Sample Resource Documents 6.8 and 6.9) to document the assistance given to the teacher. The intensive assistance plan can be the most time-consuming and frustrating part of the dismissal process and can extend into the next school year while the marginal teacher remains in the classroom, teaching children. Still, you must follow state statutes and the master contract as they pertain to an intensive assistance plan, or you will jeopardize the teacher's dismissal. Once the assistance plan is signed by all parties, the teacher cannot transfer to a different school nor can the principal change the plan. If the teacher fails to work together with the principal, the intensive assistance plan is null and void and not applicable to the next step in the dismissal process.

Sample Resource Document 7.1 is an example of an intensive assistance plan. The major sections are background information, concerns about the teacher's teaching, the teacher's plan for self-improvement, the principal's plan to assist the teacher, and the principal's final recommendation relative to the continuation of the teacher's employment in the school district. The last sentence of the plan must explicitly state that failure or unwillingness on the part of the teacher to improve his or her teaching performance may result in a recommendation for dismissal from the school district. The plan is dated and signed by the teacher, principal, and supervisor. The teacher's signature acknowledges the intensive assistance plan but does not indicate agreement.

Begin your assistance plan by recording at least five to eight concerns that you have about the teacher's teaching and include specific improvement suggestions. For example, give the teacher the opportunity to attend workshops conducted by the school district, articles to read, or a list of videotapes or CDs. You also can use the key phrases in Chapter 6 when documenting your concerns about the teacher's performance. The documentation must show that an intensive assistance plan was established and implemented for the teacher using school and district resources and that the teacher was given a reasonable length of time to improve performance. If the teacher fails to improve despite an intensive assistance plan, you will return him or her to the summative level in the evaluation process to begin the school-level dismissal meeting.

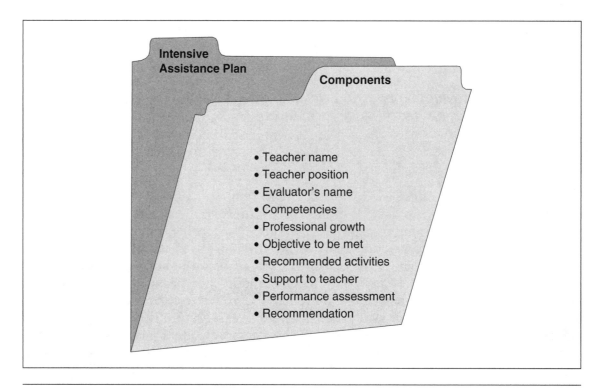

Figure 7.1 Intensive Assistance Plan

Sample Resource Document 7.1
Intensive Assistance Plan

School _____   School District _____

Teacher _____   Grade Step _____   Date Plan _____

Date Initiated _____   Date Plan Completed _____

   I. Concerns about Teaching Competencies

      A.
      B.
      C.
      D.
      E.

  II. Teacher's Plan to Improve Competencies

      A.
      B.
      C.
      D.
      E.
      F.

 III. School District Plans to Assist Teacher

      A.
      B.
      C.
      D.
      E.

Teacher's Signature _____   Date _____

Principal's Signature _____   Date _____

Supervisor's Signature _____   Date _____

 IV. Evaluator's Assessment (check one)

      ❏ Has met the expectation and timelines of the intensive assistance plan.
      ❏ Has not met the expectation and timeliness of the intensive assistance plan.

  V. Recommendation (check one)

      ❏ Recommend continuing employment, discontinuing intensive assistance.
      ❏ Recommend continuing employment, continuing intensive assistance.
      ❏ Recommend starting dismissal procedures.

Note to Teacher: *Your signature acknowledges that you are aware of your intensive assistance plan. It does not mean that you concur with the plan.*

cc: Chief Personnel Director
    Teacher
    Teacher's Representative

Getting Ready for the School-Level Dismissal Meeting

When making the decision to recommend the dismissal of the teacher, ask yourself—would I allow this teacher to teach my child?

Y ou will need to dedicate considerable time and energy to prepare for the school-level dismissal meeting to administer an unsatisfactory evaluation to the teacher. This meeting is full of twists and turns and may take many hours to complete. In fact, you may have to reschedule the meeting to another day in order to finish it. You can never anticipate everything that may occur during the meeting. You should expect the unexpected to occur and prepare for any type of attempt to block the recommendation to terminate the teacher. The teacher's representative will argue that you failed to follow the teacher evaluation process in accordance with state law or the master contract. The representative will also ridicule your documentation by referring to what was *not* done to help the teacher improve and argue that the teacher was singled out with excessive observations. Also, the teacher's representative will point out any grammatical and spelling errors in the documentation.

Planning for the Dismissal Meeting

When planning the dismissal meeting, create a seating arrangement to establish a positive businesslike atmosphere. Conduct the meeting sitting behind your desk or at the head of a conference table dressed in dark, professional attire. At this meeting, keep a copy of the master contract before you in case a question comes up about the evaluation provisions. Also, an assistant principal must attend the meeting to take notes to verify the proceedings and discussion. You should practice greeting and introducing the teacher, the teacher's representative, the teacher's supervisor, and the assistant principal or dean. Before the meeting begins, ask the teacher to identify one person, either a representative or an attorney, who will be his or her official spokesperson. Also, set the ground rules for other individuals who may be in attendance to prevent whispering, passing notes, tape recording, or videotaping. Also, cell phones and camera cell phones, pagers, and any other electronic devices must be turned off. Setting rules at the beginning will allow the meeting to proceed without major disruptions.

Dismissal Charge Statements

Each dismissal charge statement must be supported by "airtight" documentation. You must prove that the teacher failed to improve teaching performance, thereby hindering student achievement and learning opportunities in the classroom. The following charge statements will help you to compile evidence to prove the teacher is unsatisfactory and should be terminated from the school district:

- Continued pattern of unacceptable teaching
- Did not respond to efforts made to assist the teacher to improve teaching performance
- Excessive disruptions in the classroom
- Excessive student noise and movement around the classroom
- Unable to develop and teach effective lesson plans
- Failed to create an appropriate classroom atmosphere to develop the students' interest in and attitude for learning
- Failed to maintain classroom procedures for learning to occur in the classroom
- Failed to demonstrate effective teaching strategies
- Failed to maintain control of the classroom
- Failed to maintain classroom order by allowing students to randomly walk around
- Failed to create and maintain an appropriate classroom atmosphere
- Failed to develop a classroom management plan to reduce negative student behaviors
- Failed to maintain proper classroom discipline
- Failed to carry out the intensive assistance plan to improve teaching techniques
- Failed to follow suggestions and disregarded assistance to correct deficiencies in teaching
- Unable to maintain classroom control
- Unable to attain and maintain a level of acceptable teaching performance
- Unable to instruct and motivate students properly
- Inefficient in performing teaching duties
- Negatively impacted students because of poor classroom management
- Failed to improve teaching performance after being given a reasonable period of time for improvement

Prepare Opening and Closing Statements

The opening statement is the road map of how you plan to prove and support the unsatisfactory teacher evaluation. To prevent omission of important documentation, make sure that you organize the opening statement to flow in a logical sequence. During your opening statement be sure to cite the evaluation section of the state statutes, school district policy, the master contract, and reference due process; include background information about the teacher's employment in the district (including previous evaluations); and clearly state the reasons for the dismissal recommendation. You must be up front about the unsatisfactory evaluation, clearly and definitively outlining the teacher's performance strengths and weaknesses. If the teacher received average evaluations in the past, you must admit it and not hide it. In fact, you should use words from the previous evaluations, such as "a good teacher," "a team player," or "a dedicated teacher," to neutralize the teacher's representative who will use the same words to argue why he or she should *not* be terminated.

Practice reading your opening statement aloud on a tape recorder or camcorder to honestly appraise your voice to ensure that it flows smoothly without distractions—avoid awkward phrases or words, such as "umm," "um hum," "duh," "yeah," "okay," "oh," or "you know." You do *not* want to come across as being nervous by stammering, stuttering, or clamming up while presenting the unsatisfactory teacher evidence. After you present the documentation in the binder, the teacher's representative is allowed to cross-examine the evidence presented. After the cross-examination, you will read your closing statement to reiterate the reasons the teacher is recommended for dismissal from the school district. You do not have to render a dismissal recommendation at this meeting. End the meeting as agreeably as possible. You should study the evidence presented and then make a telephone call to the teacher's representative with your recommendation. Do not give a copy of your opening or closing statement to the teacher or the teacher's representative.

Actions That Should Be Completed During January and February

- Hand deliver the unsatisfactory letter to the teacher on a *Friday* afternoon, with a copy to the bargaining unit (the teacher representative). Take your assistant principal with you as a witness to the letter delivery.
- Schedule the evaluation meeting after school on a Thursday or Friday, if possible.
- Send a reminder letter to the teacher regarding the date, time, and location of the meeting.
- Draft the unsatisfactory evaluation using the district form.
- Lock the Unsatisfactory Teacher Evaluation Binder in a school file. Do not save it on your computer's hard drive.

Sample Resource Document 8.1
Letter of Intent

XYZ SCHOOL DISTRICT

ABC ELEMENTARY SCHOOL
1584 South Pine View Drive
Crescent Ridge, California 70799
(916) 444-4444

December 17, 20XX

Mr. William Anthony
ABC Elementary School

Dear Mr. Anthony:

From the beginning of September through December 20XX, formal and informal observations were made of your classroom conduct and teaching strategies. Specifically, I observed you on:

Days	Dates	Times
Wednesday	September 8, 20XX	8:00–8:25 a.m.
Friday	September 10, 20XX	10:20–10:30 a.m.
Tuesday	September 14, 20XX	1:10–1:25 p.m.
Monday	September 20, 20XX	2:15–2:30 p.m.
Wednesday	September 22, 20XX	2:45–3:00 p.m.
Monday	September 27, 20XX	8:10–8:30 a.m.
Friday	October 1, 20XX	9:15–10:10 a.m.
Wednesday	October 6, 20XX	8:05–9:00 a.m.
Tuesday	October 12, 20XX	10:15–11:05 a.m.
Tuesday	October 19, 20XX	9:10–10:20 a.m.
Monday	November 1, 20XX	9:15–10:00 a.m.
Thursday	November 11, 20XX	10:30–11:30 a.m.
Wednesday	November 17, 20XX	1:30–2:30 p.m.
Monday	November 22, 20XX	8:00–9:00 a.m.
Tuesday	November 23, 20XX	9:00–10:00 a.m.

Wednesday	December 1, 20XX	8:00–8:45 a.m.
Tuesday	December 7, 20XX	10:45–11:30 a.m.
Friday	December 10, 20XX	9:20–10:15 a.m.
Monday	December 13, 20XX	1:00–1:30 p.m.

These observations represent a reasonable sampling of your teaching performance and included all aspects of your assignment, morning and afternoon. In addition, memoranda were sent to you outlining my concerns. I held conferences with you to discuss your deficiencies, the assistance available to you, and suggestions for improvement, as well as setting a reasonable time for necessary improvement. Letters summarizing our conferences were sent to you on October 27, November 23, and December 14, 20XX. Unfortunately, at this time your teaching performance has not improved to a satisfactory step. Therefore, this letter serves as official notification that failure to achieve a satisfactory step of performance by January 14, 20XX, will result in the issuance of an unsatisfactory evaluation with a recommendation for your dismissal from the XYZ School District.

Sincerely,

Lemmie Wade, PhD
Principal

cc: Supervisor
    Calvin P. Thompson, Attorney at Law—XYZ School District

Sample Resource Document 8.2
Unsatisfactory Evaluation Letter

XYZ SCHOOL DISTRICT

ABC ELEMENTARY SCHOOL
1584 South Pine View Drive
Crescent Ridge, California 70799
(916) 444–4444

January 14, 20XX

Mr. William Anthony
ABC Elementary School

Dear Mr. Anthony:

This letter is to inform you that I plan to submit an unsatisfactory teacher evaluation for you to the Human Resources Department. I will give you a copy of this evaluation on Thursday, January 20, 20XX, at 3:15 p.m. in my office. The Master Contract, Part III, Section A, pages 15 and 16, governs the due process of teacher performance evaluations. If you wish, a member of your bargaining unit or other person of your choice may represent you during this meeting.

After the conference, you will be allowed up to 72 hours to study my comments and respond to them in writing. The unsatisfactory evaluation will then be filed with the Human Resources Department with a recommendation for your dismissal from the XYZ School District.

Sincerely,

Lemmie Wade, PhD
Principal

**Sample Resource Document 8.3
Letter Reminding the Teacher About the
Unsatisfactory Evaluation Meeting**
(Place on School Letterhead)

Date

Mr. William Anthony

ABC Elementary School

Dear Mr. Anthony:

This letter is to remind you about the evaluation meeting Thursday, January 20, 20XX, at 3:15 p.m. in my office. The purpose of this meeting is to issue you an unsatisfactory teacher evaluation. If you wish, a bargaining unit representative or a person of your choice may represent you during this meeting.

Sincerely,

Lemmie Wade, PhD
Principal

Sample Resource Document 8.4
School District Evaluation Form

Date: January 20, 20XX

Name: William Anthony   Subject/Grade: Certification K–5 Grades

School: ABC Elementary School

In my professional opinion, Mr. Anthony is not making a satisfactory contribution to the educational program for XYZ School District. The teacher exhibited some positive characteristics; however, he failed to meet teaching profession standards. It is recommended that Mr. Anthony be terminated from the XYZ School District for the following reasons:

- Continued pattern of unacceptable teaching practices;
- Inability to control students in the classroom;
- Inability to instruct and motivate students to learn;
- Failure to create an appropriate classroom learning environment; and
- Inability to obtain and maintain a level of acceptable teaching performance.

Sincerely,

Lemmie Wade, PhD
Principal

Note: Use the district evaluation form and include specific reasons why the teacher failed to meet standards of the teaching profession. Principals and other personnel delegated by position or assignment to evaluate the performance of the teacher are requested to complete the evaluation form. In the space provided, include a statement that supports the assessment.

Conducting the School-Level Dismissal Meeting

If the teacher's representative begins to attack you personally rather than attacking your documentation of the teacher, you have done a good job preparing the documentation.

Thoroughly prepare your documentation and your plan of action for conducting the school-level teacher dismissal meeting (see pp. 92–94 for a sample plan of action). You must set the guidelines to prevent confusion and establish your authority at the beginning of the meeting. After that, read your opening statement and stress that the harmful effect of the teacher's deficiencies upon student learning is the main reason for issuing the unsatisfactory evaluation. The following is a school-level narrative to guide you in conducting this important meeting.

Read Opening Statement

"The number one goal of the XYZ School District is to improve student achievement. An unsatisfactory evaluation is issued when a teacher fails to adequately respond to efforts to help improve his or her teaching performance. When a teacher fails to develop a classroom management plan that reduces negative student behavior to improve student achievement, the teacher must receive support and assistance. Mr. Anthony's inability to effectively teach greatly reduces the learning opportunities for students and negatively affects their achievement levels. I will prove in my documentation that Mr. Anthony is unable to teach and therefore his students are unable to learn in his classroom, despite the support and assistance given to him.

"This unsatisfactory evaluation is not subjective or a personality conflict with the evaluators, nor is it a result of a large number of disruptive students being unfairly assigned to his classroom. Teachers met before this school year to heterogeneously group students. Teachers, including Mr. Anthony, have input into student classroom assignment.

"The fact that the school's new reading and language textbooks did not arrive until September 21 did not prevent Mr. Anthony from teaching students successfully. In fact, other teachers in the same grade level were able to effectively teach students without the new textbooks.

"Mr. Anthony received an average evaluation from another principal at a previous school, indicating that he has classroom management problems. During my 11 formal evaluations and numerous informal observations, Mr. Anthony has been unsatisfactory in his teaching performance. In addition, the assistant principal and supervising teacher (who also conducted observations in Mr. Anthony's classroom) both provided support and assistance to him.

"Before issuance of this unsatisfactory evaluation, contractual procedures were followed to ensure that procedural and substantive due processes were applied. Part IV, Section D, on page 146 of the contract delineates the steps required by the XYZ School District master contract.

"The teacher evaluation process for the school district was communicated to all teachers in the school and the process was consistently followed. In addition:

- Mr. Anthony was not singled out; the same standards were applied to all teachers.
- Observations included all phases of Mr. Anthony's teaching assignment, morning and afternoon.
- A continuous and accurately dated file of all observations and evaluations was maintained.
- Mr. Anthony received written memoranda of concerns specifying the exact nature of his teaching deficiencies.
- Mr. Anthony received specific suggestions in memoranda of concerns for correcting these teaching deficiencies and achieving a satisfactory step of teaching performance.
- Mr. Anthony was given a reasonable period of time to accomplish necessary teaching improvements.
- Mr. Anthony was informed that failure to achieve an acceptable step of teaching performance by a certain date would result in the issuance of an unsatisfactory evaluation.
- Mr. Anthony was given opportunities for self-improvement before the unsatisfactory evaluation was issued. Mr. Anthony did not attain or maintain an acceptable step of teaching performance."

Continuation of Opening Statement

"The Department of Human Resources holds William Anthony's personnel file that contains comments about his teaching performance, including the following:

- Date: May 15, 20XX. Ms. Adele Simon—'Does not manage class well . . . needs to improve for students to learn in his classroom . . .'
- Date: April 30, 20XX. Mr. Victor Harris—'Does not have a management plan . . . kids are not learning because of poor management skills . . .'
- For the past three years, Mr. Anthony was absent for 47 school days.

School year	Days absent	Instructional time loss in hours	Absence (given in percents)
20XX–20XX	10	70.0	5
20XX–20XX	12	139.0	6
20XX–20XX	25	195.5	14
Totals	**47**	**427.5**	**25**

"Mr. Anthony's absences, as summarized for the past three years, indicate a decrease in his attendance rate of 90 percent during the last three years as compared to the average 97 percent attendance rate for teachers at this school. His attendance rate is clearly below average.

"During this school year so far, Mr. Anthony was absent 10 times for a total 70 hours of lost student instructional time. In fact, Mr. Anthony's absence rate is higher than that of students in his classroom, which averages about one day absent every two weeks.

"Numerous reasons were given for not coming to work.

Dates	Number of hours	Reasons
9/9/XX	8	Sick
9/23/XX	8	Court
9/24/XX	8	Sick
10/9/XX	8	Sick
10/12/XX	8	Sick
10/30/XX	7	Sick
11/16/XX	8	Sick
12/10/XX	8	Family illness
12/11/XX	8	Emergency
1/8/XX	8	Sick

Minutes tardy to work	Reasons
15.0	Car trouble
25.0	Overslept
10.0	Overslept
0.5	Expressway traffic
90.0	Flat tire
15.0	Personal errand
0.5	Overslept
60.0	Car trouble
15.0	Could not find car keys

"Mr. Anthony was also tardy to work nine times for a total loss of 5.7 instructional hours. Intrabuilding substitute teachers were used to cover his classes until he arrived to work, which disrupted the start of the student instructional day and placed a burden on support staff members to cover his absence in the classroom.

"In addition, Mr. Anthony has been involved in the following actions of misconduct related to teaching performance:

Date	Misconduct Charges	Disposition
10/5/XX	Leaving students unsupervised	Verbal warning
10/20/XX	Excessive use of physical force	Written reprimand
11/14/XX	Failure to report to duty	Letter in central file
12/3/XX	Undue physical force to restrain a student	Three-day suspension without pay

"Mr. Anthony filed twice for workers' compensation related to teaching performance."

School year	Claims	Dispositions
20XX–20XX	Back injury caused by an attempt to break up a student fight	Denied by Department of Human Resources
20XX–20XX	Stress caused by excessive principal classroom observations	Denied by Department of Human Resources

Pass Out the Binder

After you read the opening statement, remove the Unsatisfactory Teacher Evaluation Binder from your desk drawer and give a copy to the teacher's representative. In some cases, teachers may feel "ambushed" by the mountain of paperwork contained in the binder and may argue that it is the first time that they have been made aware of their teaching performance problems. This will negatively affect the first dismissal meeting. Nevertheless, you must present all the evidence at this time to prove the unsatisfactory evaluation. You may be unable to introduce additional documentation at the district, school committee, or arbitration hearings, and it is important that you establish that this documentation was presented to the teacher at this stage of the process (see Resource D).

The Cross-Examination

You must give the teacher's representative an opportunity to cross-examine you about the evidence presented. The following is a list of some of the questions you must be prepared to respond to:

- Where is the documentation?
- What are the negative comments?
- How many times was the class observed?
- What period was spent in the class for observations?
- What written postobservation summaries and meetings were held?
- What did you do to help this teacher?

During the cross-examination, you must never show anger toward the teacher's representative. You may find it difficult to hold your tongue and not show anger, especially if the teacher representative makes the following types of comments:

"There are two sides to this story. I feel that you're not qualified to conduct this evaluation." *Gives you a copy of a memo that you sent the teacher.* "I circled your writing errors in red ink. You misspelled the word *implement* and had several other spelling and grammar errors. As a former English teacher, I find it particularly painful to see that your memos are laced with grammatical mistakes, spelling errors, and distorted words. And you're the principal! We're talking about a superior teacher here who has always received shining evaluations from other experienced and more professional principals. He has never had any disciplinary actions against him. It's disturbing that you want to terminate this dedicated teacher. This teacher should not be terminated, you should be terminated. I'm asking you to drop this case to allow the teacher to transfer to another school next year. You do not have a case, and it will be dropped. So, let's avoid wasting all of this time and let the teacher transfer to another school."

Regardless, you must never raise your voice in anger at the teacher's representative; it will only intensify the cross-examination. However, you should not allow the teacher's representative to raise his or her voice to you or make attacks upon you. If that happens, you must stress that professional conduct is required in order for the meeting to continue. If the teacher's representative continues to act unprofessionally, you must stand up from your seat to adjourn the meeting. Follow up by sending a letter to reschedule the meeting within the contractual timeline.

Closing Statement

To end the school-level meeting, ask the teacher's representative to make a closing statement. You will make a closing statement summarizing the reasons for the unsatisfactory evaluation. An example of a closing statement follows:

> Mr. William Anthony's continued pattern of unacceptable teaching practices has had a detrimental effect on student behavior and interfered with student learning. He has been unable and unwilling to instruct and motivate students to learn and did not effectively manage his chaotic classroom. His failure to create an appropriate classroom learning environment has caused students to experience low standardized test scores. Specifically, 17 out of 28 students (61 percent) failed the state competency examination and therefore will be retained at the same grade level for the next school year. Mr. Anthony has failed to improve despite support given to help him develop his teaching performance. He failed to implement effective teaching strategies, including a classroom management plan to reduce negative student behavior in order for learning to occur in his classroom. The justifications for recommending Mr. Anthony's dismissal from the XYZ School District are the following:
>
> • Continued pattern of unacceptable teaching practices
> • Inability to control students in the classroom
> • Inability to instruct and motivate students to learn
> • Failure to create an appropriate classroom learning environment
> • Inability to obtain and maintain a level of acceptable teaching performance

Decision to Resign

Teachers have several opportunities to resign or quit before an impartial hearing body renders a negative decision about their employment in the school district. Every so often, the teacher's representative will make it known that the teacher plans to leave the school district. The principal or hearing officer must quickly work with the Human Resources Department and superintendent to call a special school committee meeting to accept the teacher's resignation to make certain that the timeline does not lapse, or the case could be lost on a technicality.

If the teacher rejects the dismissal recommendation, an impartial hearing officer must hear the case to render a decision.

Actions That Should Occur at the Dismissal Meeting in January or February

- Practice reading the opening and closing statement, including the just cause requirements.
- Review the Unsatisfactory Teacher Evaluation Binder to ensure that all appropriate documentation is included, and make a copy for the teacher's representative.
- Determine the best seating position at the conference (do not sit between teachers and their representatives). Sit at the head of the table or behind your desk.
- Conduct the unsatisfactory evaluation meeting.
- Open the meeting in a formal atmosphere.
- Have an assistant principal/dean attend the meeting to take notes.
- Have a copy of the master contract on your desk or table.
- If the teacher brings an attorney and an association representative, request that the teacher's official representative be identified before proceeding with the conference. The other individual can only observe.
- Read your opening statement.
- Distribute a copy of the Unsatisfactory Teacher Evaluation Binder to the teacher's representative.
- Present all evidence to prove the unsatisfactory evaluation at the first conference. New evidence may not be presented at the next meeting.
- Prepare for the cross-examination. Be knowledgeable about questions that might be asked by the teacher's representative, and prepare to respond to questions or criticism regarding how the teacher evaluation was conducted.

Sample Plan of Action

What the principal should do	What the principal should say
Greeting and introductions.	"Good afternoon. I don't believe we've met. I'm Lemmie Wade, the principal of ABC Elementary School. This is Robert Johnson, my assistant principal, who will be attending the meeting. The teacher's supervisor, Mr. Jonas, and central office supervisor is also in attendance."
Acknowledgment of master contract and the evaluation provisions and due process requirements.	"We are proceeding under Section IV, paragraph (D) of the master contract between the XYZ School and the Teacher's Association dated 20XX as stipulated in Part III, Section 2, on page 16 in the master contract and state statutes to evaluate unsatisfactory teachers. The teacher evaluation provisions ensure substantive and procedural due process for all teachers. This afternoon I will present evidence with regard to the unsatisfactory teacher evaluation given to Mr. William Anthony."
Pause to check for understanding.	"Do you have any questions about the meeting proceedings? Let's begin."
Teacher identifies representative.	"Mr. Anthony, who will be your official spokesperson at this meeting? No other person in attendance will be allowed to speak."
Explain the presentation order.	"Whispering, passing notes, or any unprofessional conduct is not allowed. If you need to take a break, please let me know and we can recess for 15 to 20 minutes. Are there any questions?" "I will present my documentation first. Then, you will have an opportunity to present evidence on behalf of Mr. Anthony and to conduct a cross-examination. I wish to present my documentation without interruptions."
Read the opening statement. (Do not include opening statement in the Unsatisfactory Teacher Evaluation Binder given to the teacher's representative; they are personal notes.)	"Do you have any questions?"

What the principal should do	What the principal should say
Give background information about the teacher.	"Mr. Anthony has been a teacher in the XYZ School District since August 20, 20XX, when he started teaching at King Middle School. At the beginning of the 20XX school year, he transferred to ABC Elementary School."
Make reference to teacher's certification.	"Mr. Anthony is a licensed K-8 teacher."
Make reference to teacher absence and tardiness and misconduct related to evaluation and student achievement.	"Mr. Anthony was absent 12 days out of 178 student contract days for the 20XX school year, for a total of 76 instructional hours. Mr. Anthony has filed for worker's compensation related to an accident on the school playground. Mr. Anthony has been tardy on the following dates and times. The reasons given for tardiness are car problems and traffic problems."
Make references to parental complaints.	"Parents called, e-mailed, and mailed complaint letters about the conditions in Mr. Anthony's classroom. A copy of the parental letters and phone calls regarding Mr. Anthony's classroom is included in the documentation binder."
State reason for the unsatisfactory evaluation.	"Mr. Anthony is charged with the following unsatisfactory teaching counts: • Continued pattern of unacceptable teaching practices • Inability to control students in the classroom • Inability to instruct and motivate students to learn • Failure to create an appropriate classroom-learning environment • Inability to obtain and maintain a step of acceptable teaching performance We, the evaluators, worked in concert to support and assist Mr. Anthony. I am sorry to say, we all reached the conclusion that Mr. Anthony's teaching performance is unsatisfactory."
Give representative copy of Unsatisfactory Teacher Evaluation Binder.	"At this point, I am passing out to you a copy of a binder containing the unsatisfactory teacher documentation. I will walk you through each section in the binder."

What the principal should do	*What the principal should say*
Make reference to contractual timeline.	"According to our master contract, five work days are allocated to review the information presented to render a dismissal recommendation.

The next step in the evaluation process is for an impartial hearing officer to hear the case if the teacher disagrees with the recommendation." |
Ask for clarifications.	"Do you have any questions?"
Farewell.	"Good afternoon."
Call representative.	Call the staff member's representative to let them know about the recommendation for Mr. Anthony to be relieved of his teaching responsibilities. If the staff member's representative does not agree to recommend dismissal, move the case to the next step in the master contract. You must send a letter to the teacher and teacher's representative about your decision to continue the unsatisfactory evaluation procedures, and present your case to an impartial hearing officer.

Sample Resource Document 9.1
Meeting With Hearing Officer

XYZ SCHOOL DISTRICT

ABC ELEMENTARY SCHOOL
1584 South Pine View Drive
Crescent Ridge, California 70799
(916) 444–444

Certified Mail

January 28, 20XX

Mr. William Anthony
ABC Elementary School

Dear Mr. Anthony:

In accordance with Section III, Paragraph (A), of the master contract, a conference will be held on Thursday, February 7, 20XX at 2:30 p.m. in Suite 117 at the District Administration Office before an impartial hearing officer to consider the unsatisfactory teacher evaluation.

At this conference, you are entitled to be represented by the XYZ Educators' Association or legal counsel.

Sincerely,

Lemmie Wade, PhD
Principal

cc: Supervisor
    Calvin P. Thompson, Attorney at Law—XYZ School District

10 Presenting Before an Impartial Hearing Officer/Body

You must convince the hearing officer that your documentation proves without any lingering doubt that the teacher's teaching performance is unsatisfactory.

When you are required to present the unsatisfactory teacher documentation before a hearing officer, the school committee, a review panel, or an arbitrator, you want to be sure that your case is thorough, professional, and airtight. This is your opportunity to explain how you monitored and appraised the teacher's classroom instruction and provided assistance and guidance. Teachers and their representatives may be a distraction to you while you are making a compelling argument to the hearing body. Some common strategies include blank facial expressions, not looking at you while you are talking, shaking their heads from side to side to indicate disagreement with your comments, or slovenly sitting in a chair with hands tucked under their armpits. Commit this most important concept to memory: Your main goal is to convince the impartial hearing body—*not* the teacher's representative—that the teacher is unsatisfactory and should be terminated from the school district.

The Hearing Officer

The hearing officer, an impartial body, will set the guidelines for both parties to present their case. As a rule, you will present first, followed by the teacher's representative on behalf of the teacher. You will read to the hearing officer the identical opening statement that you presented at the school-level meeting. After that, you will hand over to the hearing officer a copy of the binder containing the unsatisfactory teacher documentation. Then you will explain each section in the binder to demonstrate the support and assistance you provided to the teacher.

The following is a seating arrangement of the district-level unsatisfactory teacher evaluation:

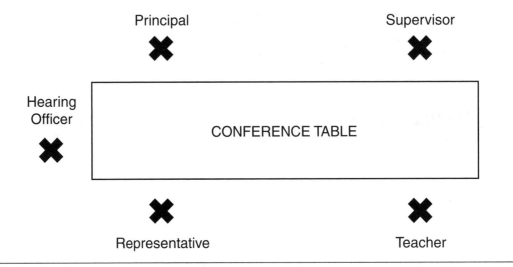

Figure 10.1   Seating Arrangement for the Unsatisfactory Evaluation Conference at the District Level

Hearing Officer's Greeting: "Good afternoon, I am Dr. Jonathon Maximus, the hearing officer for this conference."

Hearing Officer's Statement of the Purpose of Conference: "The purpose of this meeting is to hear evidence relative to the evaluation of Mr. Anthony."

Hearing Officer Acknowledgment of Contractual Provision and Due Process: "According to Section III of the master contract, the next step in the teacher evaluation process is that, under Provision III-C, an impartial hearing officer presides over the meeting to listen to testimony and review documentation and evidence before rendering a recommended resolution. In order to hear the facts at this case, it is important that all parties refrain from outbursts and use of abusive, insulting, and/or profane language directed at each other or me. There must be no disruptions during the other person's presentation. Only one person will speak at a time."

Hearing Officer States the Rules for the Meeting: "Dr. Wade will present her testimony first. Next, the teacher's representative can present testimony and/or cross-examine Dr. Wade and/or present documentation on behalf of the teacher or ask Dr. Wade questions. Are there any questions? If not, Dr Wade, you may begin."

Principal's Opening Statement: "Thank you, Dr. Maximus. Every staff member is important in the operation of ABC Elementary School. Our students deserve the best teachers in their classrooms so they can reach their greatest level of academic achievement. All teachers must have classroom management plans to provide an educational atmosphere in the classroom where students are able to learn and the teacher can effectively teach. Although the teachers' textbooks did not arrive until September 21, it did not hinder most teachers' teaching performance. This unsatisfactory evaluation is not a witch hunt or a personality conflict with the evaluators, nor was the teacher's classroom overly loaded with disruptive students. Unfortunately, Mr. Anthony was issued an unsatisfactory evaluation because he failed to respond to the efforts to improve his teaching performance and failed to develop a behavioral management plan to reduce negative student behaviors. Mr. Anthony has:

Continued a pattern of unacceptable teaching practice

Been unable to control the students in the classroom

Been unable to instruct and motivate students

Failed to create an appropriate classroom learning environment

Been unable to obtain and maintain a step of acceptable teaching performance

When this occurs, poor teaching performance has a negative impact on student achievement. Before issuance of this unsatisfactory evaluation, contractual procedures were followed to ensure that procedural and substantive due processes were applied. Part IV, Section D, page 146 of the contract delineates the steps required by the XYZ School District master contract, which were specifically followed."

Principal Reference to Due Process: "The teacher evaluation process for the school district was made known to all teachers in the school and the process was consistently followed.

"Mr. Anthony was not singled out and the same standards were applied to all teachers.

"Observations included all phases of Mr. Anthony's teaching assignment, morning and afternoon.

"A continuous and accurately dated file of all observations and evaluations was maintained.

"Mr. Anthony received written memoranda of concerns specifying the exact nature of the teaching deficiencies.

"Mr. Anthony received specific suggestions in memoranda of concerns for correcting these teaching deficiencies and how to achieve a satisfactory step of teaching performance.

"Mr. Anthony was given a reasonable period of time for necessary improvements.

"Mr. Anthony was informed that failure to achieve an acceptable step of teaching performance by a certain date would result in the issuance of an unsatisfactory evaluation.

"Mr. Anthony was given opportunities for self-improvement before the unsatisfactory evaluation was issued.

"Mr. Anthony did not attain or maintain an acceptable step of teaching performance."

Principal Background Information About the Teacher: "Mr. Anthony has been a teacher in the XYZ School District since August 20XX, when he started teaching at King Middle School. At the beginning of the 20XX school year, he transferred to ABC Elementary School. The teacher evaluation report in the XYZ personnel office indicates that Mr. Anthony received a warning about his teaching performance. The principal at King Middle School reported for two years that Mr. Anthony's teaching performance was below average. The principal states, and I quote, 'Mr. Anthony is unable to maintain a step of acceptable teaching performance resulting in a disruptive learning classroom hindering students from learning.'"

Principal Makes Reference to Teacher's Certification: "Mr. Anthony is a certified K through 8 teacher."

Principal Makes Reference to Teacher Absence and Tardiness and Misconduct File: "Mr. Anthony was absent ____ days out of _____ for the 20XX school year, for a total of _____ instructional hours. Mr. Anthony has filed worker's compensation related to an accident on school property. Mr. Anthony has been tardy on the following days and times. The reasons given for tardiness are . . ."

Principal Makes Reference to Parent Complaints: "Many parents have called and mailed complaint letters about the conditions in Mr. Anthony's classroom. A copy of the parental letters and phone calls regarding Mr. Anthony's classroom is included in my documentation."

Principal States Reason for the Unsatisfactory Evaluation: "Mr. Anthony failed to respond to the efforts made to improve his teaching performance. He has failed to develop a classroom management plan to reduce negative student behaviors. His unsatisfactory teaching performance has adversely affected student achievement. Students cannot learn in Mr. Anthony's classroom. It's too disruptive for learning to occur."

Principal Distributes Copy of Documentation: "Dr. Maximus, I am providing you with a copy of a binder containing the documentation to prove the unsatisfactory teacher evaluation. A copy of the binder was given to the teacher and his representative at the school-level conference. I will walk you through each section in the binder. The teacher representative has had several objections to documentation items. I did not remove these items. I will bring these items to your attention during my presentation."

Principal Presents Documentation to Substantiate Evaluation: "The table of contents shows the 10 major sections in the binder. I will explain the documentation in each section."

Hearing Officer Asks the Teacher's Representative to Present Argument: Give the teacher's representative an opportunity to present evidence on the teacher's behalf and cross-examine you about the evidence you presented. The representative might say, "There are two sides to this story. This is a good teacher, a veteran teacher, who has dedicated five years to successful teaching.

He has received average evaluations with numerous positive comments. I am going to ask you to drop this case so the teacher may transfer to another school next year. You do not have a case, and it will be dropped. So to avoid all of this, let the teacher transfer to another school."

Hearing Officer Asks for Closing Statements: "At this time, we will have final statements from each party. The teacher's representative will go first, followed by Dr. Wade. Each party has three minutes to present their final statements."

Principal Presents Closing Statements: "Mr. Anthony's teaching performance deficiencies are related to his failure to sufficiently manage undesirable student behavior. Mr. Anthony failed to respond to efforts that were made to help improve his teaching performance. He failed to develop a classroom management plan to reduce negative student behavior. My documentation shows beyond any lingering doubt that the teacher is unsatisfactory. I have provided negative comments about the teacher's teaching from numerous concerned parents. I conducted over 11 observations in the morning and afternoon classes. I have spent more time in his classroom than any other teacher because of his ineffective teaching and management problems. I conducted conferences, provided written post-observation summaries, and held meetings. I provided help to improve his teaching. Despite the help and assistance, Mr. Anthony has:

Continued a pattern of unacceptable teaching practice

Been unable to control the students in the classroom

Been unable to instruct and motivate students

Failed to create an appropriate classroom learning environment

Been unable to obtain and maintain a step of acceptable teaching performance

These are justifications for issuing this unsatisfactory teacher evaluation and to relieve him of his teaching responsibilities at ABC Elementary School in the XYZ School District."

The Hearing Officer May Request an Update: The hearing officer may ask for additional documentation related to the improvement and assistance that you provided to the teacher. New evidence may also be admitted as part of the teacher's unsatisfactory evaluation.

Hearing Officer Gives Clarification of the Next Step: "I want to thank both of you for your presentations and professionalism in presenting information. I will need time to evaluate the documentation presented today to render my decision. According to the master contract, I must respond within 15 workdays, but I will contact you before that time."

Hearing Officer Asks for Clarifications: "Do any of you have any questions about the next steps in the teacher evaluation process?"

Hearing Officer Farewell: "Thank you and good afternoon."

Hearing Officer Notifies You and the Teacher's Representative About the Unsatisfactory Evaluation Decision: The hearing officer has two options: recommending that the case be thrown out and that the teacher continue to be employed by the school district or recommending that the teacher be dismissed from the school district. In the latter case, the hearing officer calls you and the staff member's representative to notify both parties that he or she concurs with the recommendation for teacher's dismissal. If the staff member's representative disagrees with the decision, the hearing officer will inform him or her of the next step in the evaluation section. The hearing officer also sends a letter to confirm the recommended resolution.

Hearing Officer Contacts Human Resources Department: The Human Resources Department notifies the teacher and representative via certified mail stating that the superintendent of schools concurs with the recommendation for dismissal. The letter will also specify that a hearing will be held with the school committee to hear the teacher evaluation case.

School Committee Hearing

The Fourteenth Amendment of the U.S. Constitution outlines the rights of due process, which require a school committee to meet to hear the case for a teacher's dismissal. Simply stated, a school district cannot unfairly "deprive a citizen of life, liberty or property without due process of law." The concept of "fair play," which makes sure all teachers are treated fairly, is divided into two areas: substantive and procedural. *Substantive due process* is the fair treatment of persons by those acting under the color of laws, regulations, and policies in light of our constitutional heritage. *Procedural due process* provides for the objective dismissal of disputed questions based upon established evidence (LaMorte, 2002, p. 6).

Therefore, the teacher has the right to be represented by legal counsel and to request a public or executive hearing. A public hearing is an open meeting, while an executive hearing is only for district administrators, attorneys, the teacher and his or her immediate family, and the teacher's representative. In addition, the teacher has the right to access the evidence and the names of witnesses requested by the school committee to testify. The teacher has the opportunity to present testimony, witnesses, and other evidence, and the ability to cross-examine adverse witnesses and to present a rebuttal to the charges. The school district must provide a transcript of the hearing via a court reporter that records that the oath is taken by all witnesses and labels all exhibits presented.

It is the responsibility of the school committee president who is in charge of the hearing to explain the steps of the hearing. First, the president questions other committee members about their involvement in the case. For example, did they make any derogatory remarks about the teacher, have a phone conversation with the teacher, or have a social relationship with the teacher or the teacher's relatives? For the official record, committee members must vote "yes" to indicate that they are capable of making a fair and unbiased decision about the teacher's future employment in the district. After that, the school committee president explains the conduct expected from the participant—verbal outbursts, interrupting any presentation, or using abusive language is not tolerated. In addition, tape recorders, video recorders, cell phones, or any other electronic devices are banned from the school committee hearing. The teacher and his or her representative are seated together at one table or in one area, and the attorney for the school district, the principal, and supervisor are seated together. The witnesses are sequestered; however, the teacher may sit through the entire hearing. The president explains the presentation order for each party to present the case. The school district attorney will introduce you, the principal, as the first witness to present. It is critical that you come across as a soft-spoken, honest individual who worked hard to put together solid documentation to prove the unsatisfactory evaluation. The president will permit the teacher's representative to present testimony on behalf of the teacher or cross-examine you. Spend adequate time preparing for the hearing and practice how you would respond to the following questions:

- For the record, what is your full name and position in the school district?
- Explain your experience evaluating teachers.
- How did you make the evaluation process known to all of your teachers?
- What other positions have you held in the district?
- What written postobservation summaries and meetings were held?
- What recommendations did you make to help the teacher improve?
- What documentation do you have about the discipline problems?
- What parental complaints were made about the teacher?
- How was the evaluation process applied to all teachers?
- How did you explain the evaluation procedures to your staff?
- How many teachers did you evaluate this school year?
- How many informal evaluations did you personally conduct of this teacher?
- How many formal evaluations did you personally conduct of this teacher?
- How many suggestions did you give the teacher to improve teaching performance?

In addition, you should not be surprised if some of your staff members testify against you—especially if you spoke to them about the teacher. They may also present student and parental affidavits describing the teacher as kind, friendly, nurturing, hard working and as someone who consistently goes beyond the call of duty to help supervise afterschool activities. In closing the presentations, the school committee president will ask each party to make a two- to three-minute closing statement. The teacher's representative will present first, and the attorney for the school district will speak last. The committee will recess into an executive session to vote on the unsatisfactory teacher evaluation. If the committee votes to dismiss the teacher from the school district, the teacher has the right to file a grievance for an arbitrator to hear the case.

Grievance Proceedings

Most school districts have a three- or four-step grievance procedure for teachers to appeal an unfavorable decision. The first step begins with a hearing with the principal; the second step is a district-level hearing with a representative from the superintendent's office; and the third step is meeting with an arbitrator who renders a binding decision. Some school districts may use an appeal board to hear an unsatisfactory evaluation. The appeal board may consist of a teacher, an administrator, and a noneducator. By way of a majority vote, the appeal board could reject the school board's dismissal of the teacher and return the teacher to work in the school. In this case, the school district may be required to pay the teacher back wages, give service credit for the time missed, and pay financial damages and a judgment for emotional distress and attorney fees. In addition, the principal may have to change the evaluation to satisfactory and write a letter of apology to the teacher, promising not to retaliate. Regardless of the grievance process, the teacher can also file a lawsuit asking a judge to override the school board and/or arbitrator and reinstate him or her back to work.

A Victorious Celebration

If you followed the steps, timelines, and action items outlined in this book, you have met just cause requirements and compiled a powerful "airtight" documentation to support dismissal. As a result, an impartial hearing body will more than likely uphold the teacher dismissal recommendation despite vigorous attack by the teacher's representative. You can celebrate a victory in winning your case to remove the deficient teacher from the classroom. You have protected our most precious resources, the children, and you have done your job to make sure we have only the finest educators working with our children in the classroom. Finally, you should use any mistakes made during the dismissal process as a learning tool to begin the next school year with improved skills in your ongoing effort to remove delinquent teachers from the classroom.

RESOURCE

Sample Letters Sent to Supervisor

A.1 First memorandum to the principal's supervisor summarizing observations, conferences, and support provided to the teacher

A.2 Second memorandum to the principal's supervisor summarizing observations, conferences, and support provided to the teacher

A.3 Third memorandum to the principal's supervisor summarizing observations, conferences, and support provided to the teacher

Resource A.1
First Memorandum to the Supervisor

XYZ SCHOOL DISTRICT   ABC ELEMENTARY SCHOOL
                                        1584 South Pine View Drive
                                        Crescent Ridge, California 70799
                                        (916) 444–4444

Date: October 27, 20XX
To: Dr. Daniel Rodriguez, Supervisor
From: Lemmie Wade, Principal
Re: Potential Unsatisfactory Teacher Evaluation

During September and October 20XX, formal and informal observations were conducted in all teachers' classrooms. I observed Mr. Anthony on:

Day	Date	Time
Wednesday	September 8, 20XX	8:00–8:25 a.m.
Friday	September 10, 20XX	10:20–10:30 a.m.
Tuesday	September 14, 20XX	1:10–1:25 p.m.
Monday	September 20, 20XX	2:15–2:30 p.m.
Wednesday	September 22, 20XX	2:45–3:00 p.m.
Monday	September 27, 20XX	8:10–8:30 a.m.
Friday	October 1, 20XX	9:15–10:10 a.m.
Wednesday	October 6, 20XX	8:05–9:00 a.m.
Tuesday	October 12, 20XX	10:15–11:05 a.m.
Tuesday	October 19, 20XX	9:10–10:20 a.m.

These observations represent a reasonable sampling and included Mr. Anthony's assignment, morning and afternoon. During the postobservation conferences, Mr. Anthony's strengths and weaknesses were discussed. In addition, I offered suggestions for improvement, described the assistance available, and set a reasonable period for necessary improvement. Enclosed is a copy of the summary letter to Mr. Anthony dated October 27, 20XX, that offered specific suggestions for improvement. Also enclosed are copies of the formal and informal observation/evaluation forms used to observe Mr. Anthony. I have used the same formal and informal evaluation forms for all evaluations—the forms were presented to all teachers on September 1, 20XX, with a letter explaining the evaluation process at ABC Elementary School.

cc: Calvin P. Thompson, Attorney at Law—XYZ SCHOOL DISTRICT
    Enclosures

Resource A.2
Second Memorandum to the Supervisor

XYZ SCHOOL DISTRICT

ABC ELEMENTARY SCHOOL
1584 South Pine View Drive
Crescent Ridge, California 70799
(916) 444-4444

Date:　November 23, 20XX

To:　　Dr. Daniel Rodriguez, Supervisor

From:　Lemmie Wade, Principal

Re:　　Potential Unsatisfactory Teacher Evaluation

During November 20XX, observations were conducted in all teachers' classrooms. I observed Mr. Anthony on:

Day	Date	Time
Monday	November 1, 20XX	9:15–10:00 a.m.
Thursday	November 11, 20XX	10:30–11:30 a.m.
Wednesday	November 17, 20XX	1:30–2:30 p.m.
Monday	November 22, 20XX	8:00–9:00 a.m.
Tuesday	November 23, 20XX	9:00–10:00 a.m.

These observations represent a reasonable sampling and included all aspects of Mr. Anthony's assignment, morning and afternoon. During the postobservation conferences, Mr. Anthony's strengths and weaknesses were discussed. In addition, I offered suggestions for improvement, described the assistance available, and set a reasonable period for necessary improvement.

Enclosed is a copy of the summary letter given to Mr. Anthony on November 23, 20XX, which offered specific suggestions for improvement. Also enclosed are copies of the formal and informal evaluation forms used to observe Mr. Anthony. I have continued to use the same formal and informal evaluation forms for all evaluations—they were presented to all teachers on September 1, 20XX, in a letter explaining the evaluation process at ABC Elementary School.

cc: Calvin P. Thompson, Attorney at Law—XYZ SCHOOL DISTRICT
　　Enclosures

Resource A.3
Third Memorandum to the Supervisor

XYZ SCHOOL DISTRICT

ABC ELEMENTARY SCHOOL
1584 South Pine View Drive
Crescent Ridge, California 70799
(916) 444–4444

Date: December 14, 20XX

To: Dr. Daniel Rodriguez, Supervisor

From: Lemmie Wade, Principal

Re: Potential Unsatisfactory Teacher Evaluation

During December 20XX, formal and informal observations were conducted in all classrooms. I observed Mr. Anthony on:

Days	Dates	Times
Friday	December 1, 20XX	8:00–8:45 a.m.
Wednesday	December 7, 20XX	10:45–11:30 a.m.
Tuesday	December 10, 20XX	9:20–10:15 a.m.
Monday	December 13, 20XX	1:00–1:30 a.m.

These observations represent a reasonable sampling and included Mr. Anthony's assignment, morning and afternoon. During the postobservation conferences, Mr. Anthony's strengths and weaknesses were discussed. In addition, I offered suggestions for improvement, described the assistance available, and set a reasonable period for necessary improvement.

Enclosed is a copy of the summary letter given to Mr. Anthony on December 14, 20XX, which offered specific suggestions for improvement. Also enclosed are copies of the formal and informal evaluation forms used to observe Mr. Anthony. I have used the same formal and informal evaluation forms for all evaluations—they were presented to all teachers on September 1, 20XX, with a letter explaining the evaluation process at ABC Elementary School. I am planning to issue an unsatisfactory teacher evaluation if Mr. Anthony does not improve and would like for you to review my documentation before it is finalized.

cc: Calvin P. Thompson, Attorney at Law—XYZ SCHOOL DISTRICT
    Enclosures

RESOURCE

B

Calendar With Suggested Timeline of Actions

This sample calendar provides a visual representation of the actions in the teacher dismissal process detailed in this book. Remember, the letters and forms you use must conform to your school district standards and the master teacher contract.

August Activities

Weeks	Monday	Tuesday	Wednesday	Thursday	Friday
1					
2					Send a welcome letter to all staff members assigned to the school with the agenda for Staff Orientation Day.
3		Assign a mentor to each new teacher and identify the mentor teacher in the new teacher's welcome letter.			Provide orientation for mentor teachers assigned to assist new teachers.
4	Provide orientation for all new teachers.		Provide orientation for all staff members, highlighting philosophy, goals, expectations, and procedures (teacher/ school handbook).	Review contractual language, district policies, state statutes, and federal law regarding teacher evaluation and dismissal.	

September Activities

Weeks	Monday	Tuesday	Wednesday	Thursday	Friday
1		Prepare individual teacher files for parental complaints, samples of assignments given to students, notes and student referrals from the teacher regarding discipline problems, letters from parents, pending suspensions, and other data.	Provide a written explanation of the evaluation process with samples of evaluation instruments that will be used to evaluate the teaching staff.		
2	Begin informal observations and continue conducting observations throughout the month.		During classroom visits, collect sample assignments that teachers give to students and keep them in an individual teacher file.		
3	Inform the teacher about parental complaints as they occur and maintain a record of all complaints and communica-tion in a file.		If the quality of work samples or the teacher's classroom management is poor, write a memorandum of concerns to the teacher and include suggestions for improvement.		Provide teaching tips in the weekly staff bulletin. Discuss classroom management and other effective teaching strategies at a staff meeting.
4		Conduct informal classroom observations.		Refer the teacher to appropriate sections in the teacher handbook.	Provide teaching tips in the weekly staff bulletin.
5		Hold grade level, subject area, and committee meetings for all teachers throughout the month.			Provide teaching tips in the weekly staff bulletin.

October Activities

Weeks	Monday	Tuesday	Wednesday	Thursday	Friday
1		Conduct formal observations, provide feedback (listing areas of weakness and suggestions for improvement), and give a reasonable length of time for improvements.	Following the observations, write a memorandum of concerns listing suggestions for improvement and hold a meeting to discuss the concerns.		Conduct formal observations, provide feedback (listing areas of weakness and suggestions for improvement) and give a reasonable length of time for improvements.
2	Continue conducting daily classroom observations of all teachers.	Provide an opportunity for the teacher to observe another teacher in the same school. Provide the teacher with information on Internet sites about effective teaching strategies.	Conduct formal observations, provide feedback (listing areas of weakness and suggestions for improvement), and give a reasonable length of time for improvements.		Continue placing items in individual teacher files including parental complaints, discipline referrals, and work samples.
3	Provide teaching tips in the weekly bulletin. Refer the teacher to the weekly bulletin.	Conduct formal observation to provide follow-up suggestions and write memorandum of concerns.	Provide an opportunity for the teacher to shadow a successful teacher in another school for the entire day. Provide the teacher with information about ordering professional books and resources.	Provide the teacher with videotape that highlights successful classroom strategies and instructional techniques.	Provide an opportunity for a teacher from another school to work for a day in the teacher's classroom.
4	Prepare an Unsatisfactory Teacher Evaluation Binder with cover page, table of contents, and a divider for each section.	Request clarification about the teacher's classroom procedures.	If the teacher does not improve, issue a letter summarizing the postobservation conference. Send a potential unsatisfactory evaluation update letter to supervisor.	Conduct formal observations, provide feedback (listing areas of weakness and suggestions for improvement), and give a reasonable length of time for improvements.	Offer the teacher articles with suggestions for improvement. Check pertinent historical information about the teacher's background in the school district. Provide teaching tips in the weekly staff bulletin.

November Activities

Weeks	Monday	Tuesday	Wednesday	Thursday	Friday
1		Conduct formal observations, provide feedback (listing areas of weakness and suggestions for improvement), and give a reasonable length of time for improvements.		If the teacher is improving, note the fact on the observation form but emphasize the improvement suggestions.	Examine the teacher convention booklet to identify workshops that you recommend the teacher attend.
2	Provide teaching tips in the weekly staff bulletin.	Continue conducting daily classroom observations of all teachers. Continue collecting items for individual teacher files.	Provide the teacher with videotapes highlighting successful classroom strategies and instructional techniques.	Conduct formal observations, provide feedback (listing areas of weakness and suggestions for improvement), and give a reasonable length of time for improvements.	Send a letter to the teacher reviewing assistance provided.
3	Provide teaching tips in the weekly staff bulletin.	Offer the teacher articles with suggestions for improvements.	Videotape or audiotape the teacher's classroom and then meet with the teacher to discuss specific observations.		Conduct formal observations, provide feedback (listing areas of weakness and suggestions for improvement), and give a reasonable length of time for improvements.
4	Provide teaching tips in the weekly staff bulletin.	Issue letter summarizing the postobservation conference.	Maintain contact with the district's Department of Human Resources representative and attorney.		Send a potential unsatisfactory evaluation update letter to your supervisor.

December Activities

Weeks	Monday	Tuesday	Wednesday	Thursday	Friday
1			Conduct formal observations, provide feedback (listing areas of weakness and suggestions for improvement), and give a reasonable length of time for improvements.		Continue conducting daily classroom observations of all teachers. Provide an opportunity for the teacher to visit a classroom in the same school.
2	Provide teaching tips in the weekly staff bulletin.	Provide the teacher articles on needed areas of improvement.	Provide the teacher with videotapes highlighting successful classroom strategies and instructional techniques.	Conduct formal observations, provide feedback (listing areas of weakness and suggestions for improvement), and give a reasonable length of time for improvements.	Continue collecting information for individual teacher files.
3	Provide teaching tips in the weekly staff bulletin. Conduct formal observations, provide feedback (listing areas of weakness and suggestions for improvement), and give a reasonable length of time for improvements.	Issue letter summarizing the postobservation conference. Send a potential unsatisfactory evaluation update letter to your supervisor.	Provide opportunities for the teacher to attend workshops conducted by the school district.	Maintain contact with the district's Department of Human Resources representative and attorney.	Issue the teacher a letter stating the possibility of an unsatisfactory evaluation if the teacher fails to achieve a satisfactory step of performance. Provide teaching tips in the weekly staff bulletin.
4					

January Activities

Weeks	Monday	Tuesday	Wednesday	Thursday	Friday
1					
2	Provide teaching tips in the weekly staff bulletin. Continue conducting formal and informal observations.	Maintain contact with the district's Department of Human Resources representative and attorney.	Meet with your supervisor to discuss the unsatisfactory evaluation documentation and draft the evaluation using the district's established form.	Prepare the opening and closing statements for the unsatisfactory evaluation conference proceedings.	Review the Unsatisfactory Teacher Evaluation Binder to ensure that all appropriate documentation is included.
3	Review schoolwide discipline plan. Provide teaching tips in the weekly staff bulletin.	Prepare copies of the Unsatisfactory Teacher Evaluation Binder (one for the teacher and representative, one copy for district step representative, and one for you).			Issue the letter stating your intent to issue an unsatisfactory evaluation on Friday afternoon and send a copy to the teacher's bargaining unit.
4		Send a letter to remind the teacher about the date, time, and location of the unsatisfactory evaluation conference.	Prepare for the meeting and cross-examination. Be ready for questions that might be asked by the teacher's legal adviser.	Conduct the unsatisfactory evaluation meeting. Issue the unsatisfactory evaluation.	Provide teaching tips in the weekly staff bulletin.
5			Send the unsatisfactory evaluation form to the district's Department of Human Resources.		Provide teaching tips in the weekly staff bulletin.

February Activities

Weeks	Monday	Tuesday	Wednesday	Thursday	Friday
1		Continue conducting formal and informal classroom observations.	Prepare for presenting the unsatisfactory documentation at the next step(s).		Provide teaching tips in the weekly bulletin.
2			Continue conducting formal and informal classroom observations.		Provide teaching tips in the weekly bulletin.
3	Continue conducting formal and informal classroom observations.		Maintain contact with the district's Department of Human Resources representative and attorney.		Provide teaching tips in the weekly bulletin.
4	Continue conducting formal and informal classroom observations.	Continue conducting formal and informal classroom observations.	Continue conducting formal and informal classroom observations.	Continue conducting formal and informal classroom observations.	Provide teaching tips in the weekly staff bulletin.

March Activities

Weeks	Monday	Tuesday	Wednesday	Thursday	Friday
1		Continue conducting formal and informal classroom observations.			Provide teaching tips in the weekly staff bulletin.
2		Continue conducting formal and informal classroom observations.		Maintain contact with the district's Department of Human Resources representative and attorney.	Provide teaching tips in the weekly staff bulletin.
3	Continue conducting formal and informal classroom observations.			Present documentation at the next step in the evaluation process.	Provide teaching tips in the weekly staff bulletin.
4	Continue conducting formal and informal classroom observations.				Provide teaching tips in the weekly staff bulletin.
5					Provide teaching tips in the weekly staff bulletin.

April Activities

Weeks	Monday	Tuesday	Wednesday	Thursday	Friday
1		Continue conducting informal classroom observations.		Continue conducting informal classroom observations.	Provide teaching tips in the weekly staff bulletin.
2		Continue conducting informal classroom observations.	Continue conducting informal classroom observations.	Continue conducting informal classroom observations.	Provide teaching tips in the weekly staff bulletin.
3		Continue conducting informal classroom observations.	Begin preparing to close the school year.		Continue conducting informal classroom observations.
4	Continue conducting informal classroom observations.			Finalize teacher evaluation documentation.	Provide teaching tips in the weekly staff bulletin.
5		Continue conducting informal classroom observations.	Continue conducting informal classroom observations.		Provide teaching tips in the weekly staff bulletin.

May Activities

Weeks	Monday	Tuesday	Wednesday	Thursday	Friday
1		Present unsatisfactory evaluation documentation to the school board.	Continue conducting informal classroom observations.	Continue conducting informal classroom observations.	
2			Continue conducting informal classroom observations.		Continue conducting informal classroom observations.
3	Issue the closing school bulletin.	Complete teacher evaluations. Summarize the strengths and areas in need of improvement. Review your staff to identify potential mentor teachers and to determine staff development needs.	Complete teacher evaluations. Summarize the strengths and areas in need of improvement. Review your staff to identify potential mentor teachers and to determine staff development needs.	Complete teacher evaluations. Summarize the strengths and areas in need of improvement. Review your staff to identify potential mentor teachers and to determine staff development needs.	Complete teacher evaluations. Summarize the strengths and areas in need of improvement. Review your staff to identify potential mentor teachers and to determine staff development needs.
4	Update the closing school bulletin.		Send letters to the mentor (coach) teachers thanking them for providing support to new teachers.		

June Activities

Weeks	Monday	Tuesday	Wednesday	Thursday	Friday
1					
2					
3	Review the evaluation process.	Review state statutes, school board policy, and applicable federal laws.		Meet with teacher evaluators to review the teacher evaluation process and modify procedures as needed for the next school year.	
4	Update teacher handbook and school procedures.				
5					

RESOURCE

C

Summary Chart of
Teacher Evaluation Statutes

Internet Addresses
State Office of Education

State	Address	State Statutes	Internet Address
Alabama	Alabama Department of Education Gordon Persons Office Building 50 North Ripley Street P.O. Box 302102 Montgomery, AL 36130-2101	Secs. 16-24-1 to 13	http://www.alsde.edu
Alaska	Alaska Department of Education Suite 200 801 West 10th Street Juneau, AK 99801-1894	Secs. 14.20.009, 5-20.215	http://www.educ.state.ak.us/
Arizona	State Department of Public Instruction 1535 West Jefferson Phoenix, AZ 85007	Secs. 15-536 to 15-543	http://ade.state.az.us
Arkansas	State Department of Education No. 4 State Capitol Mall Little Rock, AR 72201	Secs. 14.20.150, 14.20.180, 14.20.205, 14.20.170	http://arkedu.state.ar.us/
California	California Department of Education Second Floor 721 Capitol Mall Sacramento, CA 94244-2720	Secs. 44932 to 44945	http://www.cde.ca.gov
Colorado	State Department of Education State Office Building 20 E. Colfax Avenue Denver, CO 80203	Secs. 22-63-103, 22-63-301, 22-63-302,	http://www.cde.state.co.us
Connecticut	Connecticut Department of Education Room 305 State Office Building 165 Capitol Avenue Hartford, CT 06106-1080	Sec. 10-151	http://www.state.ct.us/sde

State	Address	State Statutes	Internet Address
Delaware	State Department of Education P.O. Box 1402 Townsend Building Dover, DE 19903	Sec. 1401-1414	http://www.doe.state.de.us
District of Columbia	District of Columbia Department of Education 415 12th Street, N.W. Washington, D.C. 20004	Secs. 1-617.1, 1-617.3	http://www.k12.dc.us
Florida	Florida Department of Education Room PL 08 Capitol Building Tallahassee, FL 32399-0400	Secs. 16-231.29 to 16-231.36	http://www.fldoe.org
Georgia	Superintendent of Schools State Department of Education 1454 Twin Towers East Atlanta, GA 30334	Secs. 20-2-210 to 2-211, 20-2-940 to 20-2-943	http://www.doe.k12.ga.us
Hawaii	Hawaii Department of Education #309 1390 Miller Street Honolulu, HI 96813	Secs. 297-1 to 297-12	http://doe.k12.hi.us
Idaho	Idaho Department of Education Len B. Jordan Office Building 650 West State Street P.O. Box 83720 Boise, ID 83720-0027	Secs. 33-513(5) to 33-515	http://www.sde.state.id.us/Dept/
Illinois	Illinois State Board of Education 100 North First Street Springfield, IL 62777	Chap. 105 5/24-11 to 24-12, 5/24-22.4, 5.24-16	http://www.isbe.state.il.us
Indiana	Indiana Department of Education State House, Room 229 Indianapolis, IN 46204-2798	Secs. 20-6.1-4-9 to 26.1-4-14	http://www.doe.state.in.us

State	Address	State Statutes	Internet Address
Iowa	State Department of Public Instruction Grimes State Office Building East 14th and Grand Des Moines, IA 50319	Sec. 279.13-19	http://www.state.ia.us/ educate
Kansas	Kansas Department of Education 120 South East 10th Avenue Topeka, KS 66612-1182	Secs. 72-5436, 72-5447	http://www.ksbe.state.ks .us
Kentucky	Kentucky Department of Education 1930 Capital Plaza Tower 500 Mero Street Frankfort, KY 40601	Sec. 161.720-800	http://www.kde.state.ky.us
Louisiana	Louisiana Department of Education 626 North Fourth Street P.O. Box 94064 Baton Rouge, LA 70704-9064	Sec. 17-441-462	http://www.doe.state.la.us
Maine	Maine Department of Education 23 State House Station Augusta, ME 04333-0023	Title 20-A 20-1 13201-13202	http://www.state.me.us/ education/homepage.htm
Maryland	State Department of Education 200 W. Baltimore Street Baltimore, MD 21201	Secs. 6-201 to 6-203	http://www.msde.state .md.us
Massachu-setts	Massachusetts Department of Education 350 Main Street Malden, MA 02148	Secs. 71 38-42 150C 9-12	http://www.doe.mass.edu
Michigan	Michigan Department of Education Hannah Building Fourth Floor 608 West Allegan Street Lansing, MI 48933	Secs. 38.71 to 38.121	http://www.michigan .gov/mde

State	Address	State Statutes	Internet Address
Minnesota	Minnesota Department of Children, Families, and Learning 712 Capitol Square Building 550 Cedar Street Saint Paul, MN 55101	Secs. 125.12 to 125.17	http://www.education .state.mn.us/html/ 010340.htm
Mississippi	Mississippi State Department of Education Suite 365 359 North West Street Jackson, MS 39201	Secs. 37-9-59 to 37-9-113	http://www.mde.k12 .ms.us/
Missouri	Missouri Department of Elementary and Secondary Education Sixth Floor 205 Jefferson Street Jefferson City, MO 65102	Secs. 168.102 to 168.120	http://www.dese.mo.gov/
Montana	Montana Office of Public Instruction P.O. Box 202501 Helena, MT 59620-2501	Secs. 20-4-201 to 20-4-207	http://www.metnet.mt.gov/
Nebraska	Nebraska Department of Education 301 Centennial Mall South P.O. Box 94987 Lincoln, NE 68509-4987	Secs. 79-12.107 to 79-12.121.03	http://www.NDE.State .NE.US
Nevada	Nevada State Department of Education 700 East Fifth Street Carson City, NV 89710	Sec. 391.311-3197	http://www.doe.nv.gov/
New Hampshire	New Hampshire Department of Education 101 Pleasant Street Concord, NH 03301	Secs. 189:13 to 189:14-b	http://www.ed.state.nh .us/education/

State	Address	State Statutes	Internet Address
New Jersey	New Jersey Department of Education P.O. Box 500 100 Riverview Trenton, NJ 08625-0500	Title 6 Secs. 18A:6-10 to 18A:6-28, 18A:28-5	http://www.state.nj.us/ education
New Mexico	New Mexico State Department of Education Education Building 300 Don Gaspar Santa Fe, NM 87501-2786	Secs. 22-10-11 to 22-10-18	http://sde.state.nm.us
New York	New York Education Department 111 Education Building Washington Avenue Albany, NY 12234	Sec. 3012-3020-a	http://www.nysed.gov
North Carolina	North Carolina Department of Public Instruction Education Building 301 North Wilmington Street Raleigh, NC 27601-2825	Sec. 115C-325(c)	http://www.dpi.state.nc.us
North Dakota	North Dakota Department of Public Instruction 11th Floor Department 201 600 East Boulevard Avenue Bismarck, ND 58504-0440	Secs. 15-47-26 to 15-47-38	http://www.dpi.state.nd.us/
Ohio	Ohio Department of Education Room 810 65 South Front Street Columbus, OH 43215-4183	Secs. 3319.09–17	http://www.ode.ohio.gov
Oklahoma	State Department of Education 2500 N. Lincoln Blvd Room 211 Oklahoma City,OK 73105	Secs. 70 6-101 to 101.30	http://sde.state.ok.us

State	Address	State Statutes	Internet Address
Oregon	State Department of Education 255 Capitol Street N.E. Public Service Building Salem, OR 97310	Sec. 342.850–.934	http://www.ode.state.or.us
Pennsylvania	Pennsylvania Department of Education 10th Floor 333 Market Street Harrisburg, PA 17126-0333	Secs. 24-11-1122 to 24-11-1132	http://www.pde.psu.edu/
Rhode Island	Rhode Island Department of Elementary and Secondary Education 255 Westminster Street Providence, RI 02903-3400	Secs. 16-13-1, 16-13-8	http://instruct.ride.ri.net
South Carolina	South Carolina Department of Education 1006 Rutledge Building 1429 Senate Street Columbia, SC 29201	Secs. 59-25-410 to 59-25-530	http://www.myscschools.com/
South Dakota	South Dakota Department of Education and Cultural Affairs 700 Governors Drive Pierre, SD 57501-2291	Secs. 13-43-6 to 13-43-15, 13-46-1	http://www.state.sd.us/deca/
Tennessee	Tennessee State Department of Education Andrew Johnson Tower, Sixth Floor 710 James Robertson Parkway Nashville, TN 37243-0375	Secs. 49-5-501 to 49-5-513	http://www.state.tn.us/education/
Texas	Texas Education Agency William B. Travis Building 1701 North Congress Avenue Austin, TX 78701-1494	Sec. 21.001–.357	http://www.tea.state.tx.us

State	Address	State Statutes	Internet Address
Utah	Utah Office of Education 250 East 500 South Salt Lake City, UT 84111-4200	Secs. 53A-8-101 to 53A-8-107, 53A-3-411	http://www.usoe.k12.ut.us
Vermont	Vermont Department of Education 120 State Street Montpelier, VT 05620-2501	Secs. 16,1751-1752	http://www.state.vt.us/ educ
Virginia	Virginia Department of Education P.O. Box 2120 101 North 14th Street Richmond, VA 23218-2120	Secs. 22.1-293 to 22.1-314	http://www.pen.k12.va.us/ go/VDOE
Washington	Office of Superintendent of Public Instruction (Washington) Old Capitol Building 600 South Washington P.O. Box 47200 Olympia, WA 98504-7200	Secs. 28A.67.07, 0-.405.220	http://www.k12.wa.us/
West Virginia	West Virginia K–12 Schools Building 6 1900 Kanawha Boulevard East Charleston, WV 25305-0330	Secs. 18A-2-1 to 18A-2-12, 18-29-1	http://wvde.state.wv.us
Wisconsin	Wisconsin Department of Public Instruction 125 South Webster Street P.O. Box 7841 Madison, WI 53707-7841	Secs. 118.21, 118.23, 119.42	http://www.dpi.state.wi.us
Wyoming	Wyoming Department of Education Second Floor 2300 Capitol Avenue Cheyenne, WY 82002	Secs. 21-7-101 to 21-7-114	http://www.k12.wy.us/

Note: Department of education addresses, state statutes, and Internet addresses are subject to change.

RESOURCE

D

Sample Unsatisfactory Teacher Evaluation Documentation

The following sample unsatisfactory teacher evaluation documentation is provided to show the proposed organizational structure of the binder that you prepare to present the various forms and letters to substantiate the recommendation for dismissal. You may choose to modify the sequence of the sections or even some items within a section depending on your personal preference. Remember, however, that the documentation must be organized in such a way that it is easy for you to present and for the hearing officer to follow. You should use tabs to separate each major section.

A sample opening statement and a sample closing statement are also provided for your reference. These statements are your personal notes and should not be given to the teacher or the teacher's representative.

Any similarity to actual persons living or dead is purely coincidental.

Unsatisfactory Teacher Evaluation Binder

Submitted by

Lemmie D. Wade, PhD, Principal
ABC Elementary School
January 20, 20XX

Unsatisfactory Teacher Evaluation Binder

Table of Contents

I. The Beginning of the School Year

A. Welcome Staff Letter
B. Identification of a Mentor Teacher

II. Evaluation Process Made Known to All Teachers

A. Letter Identifying the Teacher's Evaluator
B. School Roster for Teachers'
    Initials Acknowledging Receipt
C. Memorandum Explaining Evaluation
    School Procedures
D. Informal Observation Form
E. Formal Observation Form

III. The Evaluation Process Applied to All Teachers

A. Monthly Staff Observations
B. Teacher Observations
C. Preevaluation and Feedback Conference

IV. Memoranda of Concerns/Memorandum of Accomplishment

A. Memorandum of Concerns No. 1
B. Memorandum of Accomplishments
C. Memorandum of Concerns No. 2
D. Improvement Suggestions

V. Teacher Assistance

A. Classroom Visit in the Same School
B. Peer Observation Form
C. Shadow Teacher at Another School
D. Teacher Visitation From Another School
E. Refer to Section in Teacher Handbook
F. Articles to Read
G. Workshops to Attend
H. Convention to Attend
I. Videotapes to View
J. Internet Sites to Search
K. Order From Publisher's Catalog
L. Read Weekly Bulletin
M. Explain Classroom Procedures

VI. Letters/Documents Relative to Assistance Provided

    A. Review of Assistance

    B. Reasonable Time to Improve

VII. Discipline Referrals

VIII. Parental Complaints

    A. Letters Informing the Teacher
About Parental Complaints

    B. Parental Complaints Filed Against the Teacher

    C. Phone and E-mail Messages

IX. Work Samples

X. Unsatisfactory Evaluation Letters and Evaluation

**XI. Failure to Achieve a Satisfactory
Step of Performance**

    A. Intent to Issue an Unsatisfactory Evaluation

    B. Letter About the Conference

    C. Complete Unsatisfactory Evaluation Form

Section I—Welcome Staff Letter

XYZ SCHOOL DISTRICT

ABC ELEMENTARY SCHOOL
1584 South Pine View Drive
Crescent Ridge, California 70799
(916) 444–4444

August 16, 20XX

Dear Staff:

I hope you are having a restful and pleasant summer vacation. As the summer rapidly closes, the 20XX–20XX school year will present new challenges to all of us—new students, new staff members, new textbooks, a new state exam, and a new technology center.

This school year, we must rededicate ourselves to helping our students reach their greatest academic potential. As always, we will work as a team to make our school the best in the XYZ School District. ABC Elementary School is the best-kept secret in the district. We are second to no other school in the district.
I am very enthusiastic about working with you to meet the challenge of educating our most precious resource, our children. Enclosed is the agenda for our first meeting. Again, welcome back! This will be the best year ever at ABC Elementary School.

Sincerely,

Lemmie D. Wade, PhD
Principal

Enclosures

ABC Elementary School
Staff Organizational Day Agenda
August 24, 20XX

8:00–8:30 a.m.	Continental breakfast, Room 114

8:30–8:50 a.m.   Welcome
Good news celebration!
New teacher introductions
New support staff introductions

8:50–10:00 a.m.   Staff orientation
Review opening day procedures
Distribution of staff handbook
Attendance procedures
Playground duty schedules
Lunch duty schedule
Specialist schedule
Librarian schedule
Specialists (e.g., counselor, psychologist)
School climate
School district discipline plan
ABC Elementary School discipline plan
Classroom management plans due September 2, 20XX
Staff evaluation procedures

10:00–11:30 a.m.   Teacher preparation

11:30 a.m.–1:00 p.m.   Lunch

1:05–2:30 p.m.   Teacher classroom preparation time

2:30–3:30 p.m.   Procedures for safe and orderly classrooms on the
first student day
• Entrance and dismissal procedures
• Lunchroom procedures
• Terminate drill and emergency procedures

Looking ahead
• First day staff meeting—August 27, 20XX
at 8:00 a.m.
• Open house—September 23, 20XX at 7:00 p.m.
• Parent-teacher conferences—October 3, 20XX

Section I—Identification of a Mentor Teacher

XYZ SCHOOL DISTRICT

ABC ELEMENTARY SCHOOL
1584 South Pine View Drive
Crescent Ridge, California 70799
(916) 444–4444

August 17, 20XX

Mr. William Anthony
4815 West Second Street
Crescent Ridge, California 70798

Dear Mr. Anthony:

Welcome to ABC Elementary School. I want you to have a professionally reward-ing and educationally successful school year. I assigned Mr. Scott Larson in Room 106 to serve as your mentor teacher for this school year. Your mentor teacher will help you with school policies and procedures and provide encour-agement and support as you create educational opportunities for your students. In addition, I can assist you in any way possible to make this a successful school year.

Again, welcome to ABC Elementary School. I am happy to have you join our staff, and I look forward to observing your enthusiasm and skill in the classroom. This will be the best year ever for our staff, students, and parents.

Sincerely,

Lemmie D. Wade, PhD
Principal

Enclosures
Organizational day agenda
cc: Mentor Teacher (coach)

Section II—Letter Identifying the Teacher's Evaluator

XYZ SCHOOL DISTRICT

ABC ELEMENTARY SCHOOL
1584 South Pine View Drive
Crescent Ridge, California 70799
(916) 444–4444

September 17, 20XX

Mr. William Anthony
ABC Elementary School

Dear Mr. Anthony:

Part III, Section A of the XYZ teacher contract states that the identification of the evaluator must be made known to the teacher by name and title by the third Friday at the beginning of the school year. I shall conduct your performance evaluation during the 20XX–20XX school year, with collaboration from other administrative and supervisory staff assigned to ABC Elementary School. In the event that someone else must serve in my capacity, that person will conduct your evaluation.

The purpose of an evaluation is to improve teaching performance and promote professional growth. This is consistent with the contract between the school committee of School Directors and the XYZ Teachers Association. The evaluation procedures for this school year will ensure that a teacher's strengths as well as weaknesses are discussed to enhance professional development to improve student achievement.

Sincerely,

Lemmie D. Wade, PhD
Principal

Section II—School Roster for
Teachers' Initials Acknowledging Receipt

ABC Elementary School
Staff Roster for Friday, September 25, 20XX

Date	Teacher Name	Teacher Signature	Room Number
	Adams, Hilda		
	Anthony, William		
	Barnett, Michelle		
	Craine, Diane		
	Elliott, Lucia		
	Haggerty, Faye		
	Hall, Rachel		
	Hernandez, Rose		
	Huebner, Shelly		
	Larson, Scott		
	Mass-Carns, Camille		
	Margis, Cindy		
	McNeal, Donald		
	Najam, Sara		
	O'Donnell, Marlene		
	Patterson, Gary		
	Thomas, Stewart		
	Williams, Darren		
	Zwicke, Gail		

Section II—Memorandum
Explaining Evaluation School Procedures

XYZ SCHOOL DISTRICT

ABC ELEMENTARY SCHOOL
1584 South Pine View Drive
Crescent Ridge, California 70799
(916) 444–4444

Date: September 15, 20XX

To: Mr. William Anthony

From: Lemmie Wade, PhD

Re: Teacher Evaluation Process

The purpose of the evaluation process is to improve teaching performance and promote the teacher's professional growth. This memorandum explains procedures that will be used to evaluate teachers this school year: the informal observation, the formal observation, and the summative evaluation. Attached is a copy of each evaluation form.

Informal Observations/Evaluations

Teachers should expect informal observations of approximately 10 to 15 minutes in length throughout the school year. A copy of the informal evaluation form will be given to the teachers after the observation.

Formal Evaluations

The school district's formal evaluation form will be used to conduct teacher observations. A formal evaluation is scheduled for the entire class period; however, it may be divided into two short observations. Teachers are to schedule an approximately 15-minute preobservation meeting with me to discuss the lesson for the day of the observation. Teachers will receive a copy of the formal evaluation form to complete a self-assessment—an honest self-assessment of their teaching. Within three to five days following the formal observation, a postobservation conference will be held to discuss the teacher's strengths, weaknesses, and improvement suggestions.

Year-End Evaluation (Summative)

The summative evaluation conference is held during April or May to evaluate school year teaching performance. The district's evaluation form will be completed and sent to the Human Resources Department to be placed in the teacher's personnel file. If you have any questions, please see my secretary to schedule a meeting to discuss the evaluation procedures.

Section II—Informal Observation Form

ABC Elementary School
Informal Observation Form

Teacher _____ Subject/Grade _____ Date _____

Time of day _____ Class period _____ Evaluation number _____

Total students assigned to class/in class _____/_____

Indicators	Satisfactory	Marginal	Needs Improvement	Unsatisfactory
1. Preparation for instruction				
2. Presentation of organized instruction				
3. Assessment of student performance				
4. Classroom management				
5. Positive learning climate				
6. Communication				

Comments _____

_____

_____

If you wish to discuss this evaluation checklist with me, please see my secretary to schedule an appointment.

Thank you,

Dr. Wade, Principal

Section II—Formal Observation Form

ABC Elementary School
Formal Observation Form

Teacher _____ Subject/Grade _____ Date _____

Time of day _____ Class period _____ Evaluation number _____

Total students assigned to class/in class _____/_____

Scale: 1 = *Outstanding*   2 = *Above average*
3 = *Average*   4 = *Fair*
5 = *Unsatisfactory*   NA = *Not applicable*

(*Note:* Insert specific criteria under the general categories, based on district standards.)

I. Planning/Instructional Strategies Used	*1*	*2*	*3*	*4*	*5*	*NA*
1.						
2.						
3.						
4.						
5.						
6.						
7.						
8.						
9.						
10.						

Comments:

II. Understanding the Curriculum	*1*	*2*	*3*	*4*	*5*	*NA*
1.						
2.						
3.						

Comments:

III. Assessment of Instructional Plan	1	2	3	4	5	NA
1.						
2.						
3.						
4.						
5.						
6.						
7.						
8.						
9.						
10.						

Comments:

IV. Classroom Management	1	2	3	4	5	NA
1.						
2.						
3.						
4.						
5.						

Comments:

V. Schoolwide Involvement	1	2	3	4	5	NA
1. List your involvement in school actions:						

Comments:

VI. Professional Development	1	2	3	4	5	NA
1. List your involvement in professional development actions:						

Comments:

Dr. Wade, Principal

Section III—Monthly Staff Observations

XYZ SCHOOL DISTRICT

ABC ELEMENTARY SCHOOL
1584 South Pine View Drive
Crescent Ridge, California 70799
(916) 444–4444

Monthly Teacher Observation Form

Attached are the monthly monitoring forms used to evaluate teachers during the 20XX–20XX school year.

_____, 20XX

Principal: _____

Insert the names of all teachers in the first column, and add the dates in the section on the top column. Place the code in the grid to indicate the type of observation conducted.

Table key: WT: Walk Through
IE: Informal Evaluation
FE: Formal Evaluation

Teachers																

Section III—Teacher Observations

XYZ SCHOOL DISTRICT

ABC ELEMENTARY SCHOOL
1584 South Pine View Drive
Crescent Ridge, California 70799
(916) 444–4444

CLASSROOM OBSERVATIONS OF MR. WILLIAM ANTHONY

Observations of Mr. Anthony's classroom included all phases of his assignment, morning and afternoon. He was not singled out; all other teachers at this school were comparably evaluated. Thirty-six classroom observations—informal and formal—were conducted of Mr. William Anthony's classroom.

Informal Observations	25
Formal Observations	11
Total observations	36

Section III—Preevaluation and Feedback Conference

XYZ SCHOOL DISTRICT

ABC ELEMENTARY SCHOOL
1584 South Pine View Drive
Crescent Ridge, California 70799
(916) 444–4444

LETTERS SUMMARIZING MEETINGS FOLLOWING CLASSROOM OBSERVATIONS

Next are the letters issued to Mr. William Anthony summarizing meetings held with him to discuss concerns about his teaching performance.

October 27, 20XX

December 14, 20XX

XYZ SCHOOL DISTRICT

ABC ELEMENTARY SCHOOL
1584 South Pine View Drive
Crescent Ridge, California 70799
(916) 444–4444

October 27, 20XX

Mr. William Anthony
ABC Elementary School

This letter is a summary of the meeting held in my office on Friday, October 22, 20XX, at 3:30 p.m. to discuss your teaching performance. I began the meeting stating the following concerns about your inability to manage a classroom:

1. Lack of an effective classroom management plan
2. Failure to develop quality lesson plans
3. Failure to maintain class control
4. Lack of classroom procedures
5. Failure to respond consistently to student misbehaviors
6. Ineffective student seating arrangement causing problems
7. Unappealing, lackluster, and tattered room bulletin boards

I discussed the support materials and opportunities provided to help you to improve your teaching. I provided you the following materials, suggestions, and visitation opportunity at another school:

1. Two articles to read about classroom management
2. An effective teaching videotape to view
3. Opportunities to attend workshops on classroom management, teaching, and cooperative learning for small group instruction
4. A copy of pages from the teacher handbook about lesson plans, the homework policy, schoolwide rules and consequences, and student discipline
5. Suggestions to change your student seating arrangement to allow you to more effectively monitor the entire class
6. Suggestions to post classroom rules, consequences, and rewards
7. The opportunity to observe classroom management, organizational skills, and instructional techniques of a veteran teacher

I will continue to support you to improve your teaching effectiveness and classroom management skills. However, the effort must come primarily from you to improve your teaching performance.

Sincerely,

Lemmie Wade, PhD
Principal

Attachments

XYZ SCHOOL DISTRICT

ABC ELEMENTARY SCHOOL
1584 South Pine View Drive
Crescent Ridge, California 70799
(916) 444–4444

December 14, 20XX

Mr. William Anthony
ABC Elementary School

Dear Mr. Anthony:

This is the letter summarizing the second meeting held with you in my office on Wednesday, November 10, 20XX, at 3:30 p.m. I began the meeting discussing what progress you had made to improve your teaching performance. Again, I stated the following concerns about your inability to teach and manage your classroom:

1. Lack of effective classroom management skills

2. Failure to prepare quality lesson plans to teach a lesson

3. Failure to respond consistently to student misbehavior

4. Failure to manage escalating off-task student behavior in lesson transition

5. Lack of classroom procedures

We also discussed support materials and the opportunity to visit at another school. I also gave you the following suggestions to improve your teaching and classroom management skills:

1. View video on preparing lesson plans

2. Review the teacher handbook sections on report cards, parent complaints, and communication strategies for parent-teacher conferences

3. Establish clear classroom procedures for students

4. Increase your mobility to effectively monitor students during practice and do not sit behind your desk

I am available to assist you in improving your teaching effectiveness. However, failure to improve your teaching performance by January 14, 20XX, may result in an unsatisfactory teacher evaluation.

Sincerely,

Lemmie Wade, PhD
Principal

Section IV—Memorandum of Concerns No. 1

XYZ SCHOOL DISTRICT   ABC ELEMENTARY SCHOOL
                                       1584 South Pine View Drive
                                       Crescent Ridge, California 70799
                                       (916) 444–4444

Two Memoranda of Concerns were issued to Mr. Anthony about his teaching performance. Each memo listed suggestions to improve his teaching performance.

XYZ SCHOOL DISTRICT

ABC ELEMENTARY SCHOOL
1584 South Pine View Drive
Crescent Ridge, California 70799
(916) 444–4444

Date: October 1, 20XX

To: Mr. William Anthony

From: Dr. Lemmie Wade

Re: Memorandum of Concerns No. 1

During the past month, numerous informal and formal evaluations were conducted of your classroom teaching. I gave you a copy of my evaluations. In addition, postobservation meetings were held with you to discuss suggestions to improve your teaching performance. This memorandum reiterates the need for you to have an effective classroom management plan in order to successfully teach students. As a follow-up to this memorandum, I will conduct another evaluation using a memorandum of accomplishment to assess your progress in line with the suggestions and guidance you have been provided.

*Concern 1—*Classroom Management Procedures

Your classroom is an unsafe student-learning environment. I feel there is little or no learning taking place in your classroom because there are no rules, consequences, rewards, or procedures. For example, on Thursday, September 26, 20XX, at approximately 10:10 a.m., I observed students wandering around the room talking to each other while you stood in one place in front of the class. Some students were shouting out answers, and other students were yelling at other classmates to be quiet. You sent three students to the office for talking out of turn. By noon, you had sent 10 students to the office for minor infractions (talking out of turn, not having supplies, walking around the room, and chewing gum).

Improvement Suggestions

1. Develop a classroom management plan to handle minor student behaviors.

2. Post your classroom management plan (e.g., rules, consequences, rewards).

3. Use good work as a reward (e.g., computer time, free time).

4. Develop a flyer, brochure, or letter to inform parents about your classroom management plan.

5. Develop clear classroom procedures and routines.

6. Develop nonverbal strategies to get student attention (e.g., firm look, hand clap, light signal, hand or finger sign).

7. Give your students options to choose consequences for their behavior.

8. Make sure the sanctions for misbehavior are punishing in nature and are not considered fun.

9. Do not send students to the office for minor infractions (e.g., chewing gum, not having a pencil).

10. Report major problems to the principal.

11. After each break (e.g., winter recess, spring break, track break), rehearse classroom rules and procedures with students.

Concern 2—Classroom Management (Morning Procedures)

You must pick up your students on the playground on time at the start of the school day to escort them quietly to the classroom. As you know, a warning bell rings at 8:50 a.m. for teachers to pick up their students in ten minutes—9:00 a.m. For example, on Friday, September 15, 20XX, your students were left unsupervised on the playground for eight minutes, which resulted in a student fight. When you did come to retrieve your students, you yelled at them, "Stop it, stop it!" If you had been on time, your presence may have prevented this fight. You must be a proactive teacher to prevent potential problems.

Improvement Suggestions

1. Arrive by 8:58 a.m. to greet and pick up students on the playground.

2. Develop procedures for walking in the corridor (e.g., arrival, recess, lunch, dismissal).

3. Assign a student line monitor to lead the students into the school.

4. Know the names of your students so you can talk with them in the morning on the playground.

5. Start the school day by providing a safe and orderly climate in which children can learn.

6. Develop a plan to handle potential early-morning troublemakers.

7. Explain the reason for punishment for misbehavior, but refrain from saying, "If you don't behave in line, the whole class will stay in for recess."

8. Refrain from bluffing students about what you will do if they misbehave if you're unable to follow through with the consequences.

9. React calmly and quickly to discipline problems.

Concern 3—Classroom Management (Beginning Morning Actions)

You must establish morning learning routines to get the class off to a good start. For example, I have observed students running in and out of your classroom on several occasions. You are lacking a plan or procedure to get your students started every school day in an orderly and productive manner.

Improvement Suggestions

1. Develop morning routines to get your class off to a good start.

2. Post a daily schedule and discuss any changes each morning. Include art, music, physical education, and any pullout programs in this schedule.

3. Account for every minute in the school day.

4. Give clear systematic directions to students.

5. Arrange seating so you can see the children and, if necessary, move them to different seat locations.

6. Design a floor plan for small group activities.

7. Relocate your bookcases to establish clear traffic patterns.

8. Design learning centers for computers, reading, mathematics, and so forth.

9. Keep learning center tables organized and stocked with necessary materials.

10. Do not allow troublemakers to sit together.

11. Develop a plan for handling playground equipment for recess and lunchtime.

12. Refrain from telling students that they will not be allowed to return to your classroom.

13. Do not allow students to wander around the classroom.

14. Do not allow students to throw crayons in the classroom.

In closing, this memorandum of concerns describes my apprehension about your teaching performance and offers more than 30 improvement suggestions. I gave you a copy of each evaluation and held postobservation meetings to discuss suggestions to improve your teaching performance. Again, I stand ready to support you in improving your teaching performance, but the effort must come from you. Please contact my secretary to schedule a meeting if you wish to discuss this memorandum of concerns. At this meeting, you may be represented by a teachers' association representative or other person of your choice.

Section IV—Memorandum of Accomplishments

XYZ SCHOOL DISTRICT

ABC ELEMENTARY SCHOOL
1584 South Pine View Drive
Crescent Ridge, California 70799
(916) 444–4444

Date: October 31, 20XX
To: Mr. William Anthony
From: Dr. Lemmie Wade, Principal
Re: Accomplishment of Suggestions for Teaching Improvement

A Memorandum of Concerns was sent to you on October 1, 20XX, listing concerns about your teaching. This is a Memorandum of Accomplishments to assess your progress toward achieving the teaching improvements suggested in the first memo. I used the rating scale below in my assessment of your teaching improvements:

1. Unsatisfactory Accomplishment
2. Marginal Accomplishment
3. Satisfactory Accomplishment
4. Above Average Accomplishment
5. Excellent Accomplishment

Concern 1—Classroom Management Procedures

Your classroom is an unsafe student-learning environment. I feel there is little or no learning taking place in your classroom because there are no rules, consequences, rewards, or procedures. For example, on Thursday, September 26, 20XX, at approximately 10:10 a.m., I observed students wandering around the room talking to each other while you stood in one place in front of the class. Some students were shouting out answers and other students were yelling at other classmates to be quiet. You sent three students to the office for talking out of turn. By noon, you had sent 10 students to the office for minor infractions (talking out of turn, not having supplies, walking around the room, and chewing gum).

Improvement Suggestions	*Accomplishment of Suggestions*
1. Post a classroom management plan to handle minor student behaviors.	1
2. Post your classroom management plan (e.g., rules, rewards, consequences).	2
3. Use good work as a reward (e.g., computer time, free time).	1
4. Develop a flyer, brochure, or letter to inform parents about your classroom management plan.	2
5. Develop clear classroom procedures and routines.	1

Improvement Suggestions	Accomplishment of Suggestions
6. Develop nonverbal strategies to get student attention (e.g., firm look, hand clap, light signal, hand or finger sign).	1
7. Give your students options to choose consequences for their behavior.	1
8. Make sure the sanctions for misbehavior are punishing in nature and are not considered fun.	1
9. Do not send students to the office for minor infractions (e.g., chewing gum, not having a pencil).	1
10. Report major problems to the principal.	1
11. After each break (e.g., winter recess, spring break, track break), rehearse classroom rules and procedures with students.	1

Concern 2—Classroom Management (Morning Procedures)

You must pick up your students on the playground on time at the start of the school day to escort them quietly to the classroom. As you know, a warning bell rings at 8:50 a.m. for teachers to pick up their students in ten minutes—9:00 a.m. For example, on Friday, September 15, 20XX, your students were left unsupervised on the playground for eight minutes, which resulted in a student fight. When you did come to retrieve your students, you yelled at them, "Stop it, stop it!" If you had been on time, your presence may have prevented this fight. You must be proactive teacher to prevent potential problems.

Improvement Suggestions	Accomplishment of Suggestions
1. Arrive by 8:58 a.m. to greet and pick up students on the playground.	2
2. Develop procedures for walking in the corridor (e.g., arrival, recess, lunch, dismissal).	2
3. Assign a student line monitor to lead the students into the school.	2
4. Know the names of your students so you can talk with them in the morning on the playground.	2
5. Start the school day by providing a safe and orderly climate in which children can learn.	2
6. Develop a plan to handle potential early-morning troublemakers.	1
8. Refrain from bluffing students about what you will do if they misbehave if you're unable to follow through with the consequences.	1
9. React calmly and quickly to discipline problems.	1

Concern 3—Classroom Management (Beginning Morning Actions)

You must establish morning learning routines to get the class off to a good start. For example, I have observed students running in and out of your classroom on several occasions. You are lacking a plan or procedure to get your students started every school day in an orderly and productive manner.

Improvement Suggestions	*Accomplishment of Suggestions*
1. Develop morning routines to get your class off to a good start.	2
2. Post a daily schedule and discuss any changes each morning. Include art, music, physical education, and any pullout programs in this schedule.	1
3. Account for every minute in the school day.	1
4. Give clear systematic directions to students.	2
5. Arrange seating so you can see the children and, if necessary, move them to different seat locations.	1
6. Design a floor plan for small group activities.	1
7. Relocate your bookcases to establish clear traffic patterns.	2
8. Design learning centers for computers, reading, mathematics, and so forth.	1
9. Keep learning center tables organized and stocked with necessary materials.	2
10. Do not allow troublemakers to sit together.	2
11. Develop a plan for handling playground equipment for recess and lunchtime.	2
12. Refrain from telling students that they will not be allowed to return to your classroom.	1
13. Do not allow students to wander around the classroom.	1
14. Do not allow students to throw crayons in the classroom.	1

Although you have made a few teaching changes, your teaching performance, in my opinion, it is still unsatisfactory. You must successfully implement the other teaching suggestions as specified in the first memorandum of concerns. I will continue to conduct informal and formal observations to evaluate your teaching performance. I want to be as clear as possible that if your teaching performance does not improve within the next 20 school days, you may receive an unsatisfactory teacher evaluation. If you have questions about this memorandum, you can write a letter within the next 10 school days or you can see my secretary to schedule a meeting with me to discuss the memorandum. At this meeting, you may be represented by anyone of your choice.

Note: The Memorandum of Accomplishments must include the concerns and suggestions mentioned in the Memorandum of Concerns.

Section IV—Memorandum of Concerns No. 2

XYZ SCHOOL DISTRICT

ABC ELEMENTARY SCHOOL
1584 South Pine View Drive
Crescent Ridge, California 70799
(916) 444–4444

Date: November 4, 20XX

To: Mr. William Anthony

From: Lemmie Wade, PhD

Re: Memorandum of Concerns No. 2

This is the second Memorandum of Concerns sent to you with regard to improving your teaching effectiveness. I will state my concerns and offer suggestions to improve your teaching performance. Although you have shown some improvement, you must address classroom management and improve your teaching strategies so that effective learning will occur in your classroom.

Concern 1—Having an Unattractive Classroom

As stated earlier, I am concerned about the appearance of your classroom. A bulletin board should be changed periodically to reflect the seasons as well as to display successful schoolwork.

Suggestions:

1. Use attractive colors on the bulletin boards to reflect the fall season.
2. Display schoolwork of your students.
3. Remove pencil and crayon marks from desks and floors.
4. Post your classroom management plan on a bulletin board.
5. Develop a procedure for cleaning the floor of paper and trash.

Concern 2—Ineffective Teaching Strategies

Suggestions:

1. Develop lesson plans for each subject area.
2. Design your plan in a clear, logical, and sequential format.
3. To capture student attention, begin the lesson with a motivational activity.
4. Make the objective of the lesson known to students.
5. Maintain good momentum (pacing) to keep students involved.
6. Use a variety of questioning steps and give students many opportunities to respond.

7. Check periodically for student comprehension of concepts.

8. Be more mobile in the classroom and do not stand in one location.

9. Use examples that students can understand.

10. Keep students involved in the lesson.

11. Reinforce appropriate student behavior.

12. Provide challenging seatwork related to the subject area being learned.

13. Make a smooth transition between actions.

14. Praise students for good work.

15. Use a variety of teaching strategies.

16. Develop a procedure for students to signal you when they need help.

17. Develop procedures for students who finish their work early.

18. Develop procedures for assigning students to cooperative groups.

In closing, I want you to know that I support you as a classroom teacher, but the responsibility to improve your teaching rests directly with you. Because of the importance of this matter, we must meet to discuss this memorandum of concerns and to outline a specific timeline for improvements to occur in your classroom. Please see my secretary to arrange a date and time for this meeting. At this meeting, you may be represented by a teachers' association representative or other person of your choice.

Section IV—Improvement Suggestions

XYZ SCHOOL DISTRICT

ABC ELEMENTARY SCHOOL
1584 South Pine View Drive
Crescent Ridge, California 70799
(916) 444–4444

November 27, 20XX

Mr. William Anthony
ABC Elementary School

Dear Mr. Anthony:

During the past 10 weeks, I have made suggestions to help you improve your teaching performance in the following areas:

- Classroom Organization and Procedures
  Physical organization
  Expectations
  Grading system

- Learning Environment
  Positive teacher-student interaction
  Rewards and encouragement
  Multicultural awareness

- Lesson Planning and Presentation
  Introduction
  Motivation
  Organization
  Closure
  Assessment

- Instructional Techniques
  Cooperative learning
  Reading instruction
  Mathematics instruction

- Student Discipline
  Conflict resolution
  Assertive discipline

I would like to meet with you to discuss these suggestions for improvement and the progress that you have made. Please contact my secretary to schedule an appointment with me.

As always, I stand ready to assist you in making this school year a successful teaching experience.

Sincerely,

Lemmie Wade, PhD
Principal

Section V—Classroom Visit in the Same School

XYZ SCHOOL DISTRICT

ABC ELEMENTARY SCHOOL
1584 South Pine View Drive
Crescent Ridge, California 70799
(916) 444–4444

October 7, 20XX

Mr. William Anthony
ABC Elementary School

Dear Mr. Anthony:

I would like you to visit Mr. Scott Larson's classroom to observe his classroom management procedures and instructional techniques for small and large group instruction. Arrangements have been made for a substitute to teach your class on Monday, October 11, 20XX, from 9:30 to 11:00 a.m.

During the observation, use the attached Peer Observation Form to learn how Mr. Larson operates his classroom. Pay attention to his rules, procedures, routines, classroom seating arrangement, cooperative grouping learning, teaching skills, lesson closure, and transitions between lessons.

Again, I stand ready to assist you in making this school year a successful teaching experience. We will discuss the observation at our next meeting on November 1 at 3:30 p.m. in my office.

Sincerely,

Lemmie Wade, PhD
Principal

Enclosure

Section V—Peer Observation Form

ABC Elementary School
Peer Observation Form

I. Starting the school day

1. How did the teacher escort students to the classroom?
2. How did the teacher greet the students?
3. What communication took place between the teacher and students? (positive or negative, friendly or neutral, personal or general, etc.)
4. What opening-the-school-day actions occurred in the classroom? Were they planned or on-the-spot decisions? Were the actions work or fun? Was a time limit set?
5. How did the teacher take attendance? (Using the seating chart? By homework turned in? Other system?)
6. How did the teacher collect money (lunch/supply/field trip)?

II. Classroom Management

1. What was the teacher's classroom management plan?
2. What classroom management strategies were used to operate the classroom?
3. What features reflected the teacher's enthusiasm (i.e., vocal delivery, eye movement, gestures, body movement, facial expression, word selection, acceptance of ideas and feelings, and overall energy)?

III. Classroom Instruction

1. How did the teacher begin the lesson with a motivational activity to capture student attention?
2. How did the teacher make the objective known to students?
3. How was the instructional material presented?
4. How did the teacher begin the lesson quickly?
5. How were students required to participate?
6. How did the teacher keep the students motivated during the lesson?
7. How did the teacher use good examples?
8. How did the teacher use a variety of questions?
9. How mobile was the teacher?
10. Did the teacher stand in one location or move around?
11. How did the teacher close the lesson?
12. How was student work collected?
13. How did the teacher assign homework?

IV. Assessment

1. What strategies did the teacher use that could help you improve your teaching?
2. What worked well? What did not work well?
3. What insights have you gained from observing this teacher?

Section V—Shadow Teacher at Another School

XYZ SCHOOL DISTRICT

ABC ELEMENTARY SCHOOL
1584 South Pine View Drive
Crescent Ridge, California 70799
(916) 444–4444

October 19, 20XX

Mr. William Anthony
ABC Elementary School

Dear Mr. Anthony:

As we have discussed earlier, opportunities are available for teachers to observe classes and teachers in other schools in our district. I have arranged for you to spend a day at Redwood Elementary School, which is located at 8439 West Redwood Drive.

You are to report to the school office to meet with Mrs. Beverly Martinez, Principal at Redwood School, at 8:00 a.m. Tuesday, October 27, 20XX. You will spend the day observing in Mr. David Riley's fifth grade classroom. He is an experienced teacher who has excellent classroom management skills as well as instructional techniques. If you believe it would be worthwhile, I can arrange to have Mr. Riley visit your classroom, too.

Again, I stand ready to assist you in making this a successful teaching experience.

Sincerely,

Lemmie Wade, PhD
Principal

Section V—Teacher Visitation From Another School

XYZ SCHOOL DISTRICT

ABC ELEMENTARY SCHOOL
1584 South Pine View Drive
Crescent Ridge, California 70799
(916) 444–4444

November 5, 20XX

Mr. William Anthony
ABC Elementary School

Dear Mr. Anthony:

I was pleased that your visit to Redwood Elementary School was a helpful professional experience. I have made arrangements for Mr. David Riley, a fifth-grade teacher from Redwood Elementary School, to spend the entire school day in your classroom on Monday, November 15, 20XX. During that time, Mr. Riley can work with you to improve your teaching and classroom management skills.

Again, I stand ready to assist you in making this school year a successful teaching experience.

Sincerely,

Lemmie Wade, PhD
Principal

Section V—Refer to Section in Teacher Handbook

XYZ SCHOOL DISTRICT

ABC ELEMENTARY SCHOOL
1584 South Pine View Drive
Crescent Ridge, California 70799
(916) 444–4444

September 23, 20XX

Mr. William Anthony
ABC Elementary School

Dear Mr. Anthony:

At the beginning of the school year, you received a copy of the ABC Elementary School Teacher Handbook. This handbook contains information to clarify rules and procedures to ensure the smooth operation of our school. All teachers are responsible for knowing the procedures in the handbook. Below are the sections in the handbook that will help you to improve your teaching performance. Please review the following sections:

Section	*Description*
IV	Effective Instructional Strategies
V	School Procedures
VI	Classroom Management

I stand ready to assist you in making this a successful school year.

Sincerely,

Lemmie Wade, PhD
Principal

Enclosures—Teacher Handbook Overview and Table of Contents

Note: Include a copy of the pages cited in the handbook when preparing the Unsatisfactory Teacher Evaluation Binder.

ABC Elementary School

Teacher Handbook

20XX–20XX

TEACHER HANDBOOK OVERVIEW

The ABC Elementary School Teacher Handbook is organized into six sections to provide information on the overall school operation. Section I includes the school calendar, schedule of events, and a school directory. Section II includes the school philosophy, mission statement, and goals. Section III includes information about ABC's administration and staff and the school decision-making model. Section IV includes the curriculum, instructional strategies, lesson planning, and classroom management. Section V includes school safety and emergency procedures, such as fire drills, tornadoes, and in-school safety drills. Section VI outlines classroom management and contains effective classroom teacher strategies. Section VII includes information about staff evaluation procedures.

TEACHER HANDBOOK

TABLE OF CONTENTS

A message from the principal

Section I: School Calendar and Events

School calendar
Schedule of events
School directory
School map
Bell schedule
Room assignments
Specialist assignments (guidance, social worker, psychologist)

Section II: School Philosophy

School committee goals and objectives
School committee members
District goals

Section III: School Administration

Administrators' duties
School operational model
School leadership council
School committees

Section IV: Effective Instructional Strategies

Curriculum allocations
Lesson plans
Classroom management

Section V: School Procedures

Weekly bulletin
Daily bulletin
Field trips
School bus
Fire drills
Tornado drills
Crisis drills
Emergency closing
Lunchroom

Assemblies
Audio-visual equipment
Supplies and equipment
Purchase requisitions
Substitute teachers
Safety plan
School meetings: attendance and expectations
Duty roster, bus, lunchroom, bulletin boards
Arrival and dismissal
Forms
Visitors to building
Volunteer job descriptions
Acceptable staff behavior
Tips to reduce staff/student conflict
Confidentiality of records
Student attendance
Lockers
Grading
School safety
Afterschool detention
Dress code
Homework policy
Health records
Cumulative folders
Health and special education students
Promotion/retention policy

Section VI: Classroom Management

Discipline policy of district and school
Classroom organization
Classroom rules
School rules
School district rules
Student discipline
Student referral procedures

Section VII: Staff Evaluation

Teachers
Specialists
Educational assistants

Appendix

Section V—Articles to Read

XYZ SCHOOL DISTRICT

ABC ELEMENTARY SCHOOL
1584 South Pine View Drive
Crescent Ridge, California 70799
(916) 444–4444

October 22, 20XX

Mr. William Anthony
ABC Elementary School

Dear Mr. Anthony:

Enclosed you will find copies of the following articles, which should help you to improve your classroom management and teaching techniques:

1. "Proactive Teaching Strategies"

2. "Basic Classroom Management"

3. "The Good Teacher"

4. "A Teacher Making/Made the Difference"

As always, I stand ready to assist you in making this school year a successful teaching experience.

Sincerely,

Lemmie Wade, PhD
Principal

Enclosures

Note: Include a copy of all articles in the Unsatisfactory Teacher Evaluation Binder.

XYZ SCHOOL DISTRICT

ABC ELEMENTARY SCHOOL
1584 South Pine View Drive
Crescent Ridge, California 70799
(916) 444–4444

November 16, 20XX

Mr. William Anthony
ABC Elementary School

Dear Mr. Anthony:

Attached are copies of articles to help you to improve your classroom management and teaching techniques. They are:

1. "Creating a Positive Classroom Learning Experience"

2. "How to Prepare an Effective Reading Lesson"

3. "Discipline—A Step-by-Step Guide for Elementary School Teachers"

As always, I stand ready to assist you in making this school year a successful teaching experience.

Sincerely,

Lemmie Wade, PhD
Principal

Enclosures

Note: Include a copy of all articles in the Unsatisfactory Teacher Evaluation Binder.

Section V—Workshops to Attend

XYZ SCHOOL DISTRICT

ABC ELEMENTARY SCHOOL
1584 South Pine View Drive
Crescent Ridge, California 70799
(916) 444–4444

October 20, 20XX

Mr. William Anthony
ABC Elementary School

Dear Mr. Anthony:

The XYZ School District's Fall 20XX Staff Development Bulletin lists several inservice classes that might be beneficial to improve your classroom teaching performance. I want you to enroll in the following classes:

- Classroom Management
- Teaching Reading in the Intermediate Grades
- Cooperative Learning

As always, I stand ready to assist you in making this a successful teaching experience. The head secretary in the school office has the registration forms.

Sincerely,

Lemmie Wade, PhD
Principal

Enclosures

Note: Include a copy of all articles in the Unsatisfactory Teacher Evaluation Binder.

XYZ SCHOOL DISTRICT

ABC ELEMENTARY SCHOOL
1584 South Pine View Drive
Crescent Ridge, California 70799
(916) 444–4444

December 15. 20XX

Mr. William Anthony
ABC Elementary School

Dear Mr. Anthony:

The XYZ School District Spring 20XX Staff Development Bulletin lists several inservice classes that would be beneficial to your classroom teaching performance. I suggest that you enroll in the following classes:

- Reading in the Content Areas
- Assertive Discipline
- Survival Skills for the Classroom Teacher

As always, I stand ready to assist you in making this a successful teaching experience. The head secretary in the school office has the registration forms.

Sincerely,

Lemmie Wade, PhD
Principal

Enclosures

Note: Include a copy of all articles in the Unsatisfactory Teacher Evaluation Binder.

Section V—Convention to Attend

XYZ SCHOOL DISTRICT

ABC ELEMENTARY SCHOOL
1584 South Pine View Drive
Crescent Ridge, California 70799
(916) 444–4444

November 2, 20XX

Mr. William Anthony
ABC Elementary School

Dear Mr. Anthony:

The XYZ Teachers' Convention will be held from November 4 to 5, 20XX, at the Metropolitan Convention Center. The convention booklet lists several workshops that should assist you in improving your teaching performance. I suggest that you attend the following workshops:

Title	Date	Time	Room
Conflict Resolution	11/4/XX	9:00 a.m.	Renaissance
Classroom Management	11/4/XX	11:00 a.m.	Van Gogh
New Instructional Strategies	11/4/XX	2:30 p.m.	Rembrandt
Cooperative Learning	11/5/XX	9:30 a.m.	Van Gogh
Multicultural Awareness	11/5/XX	11:00 a.m.	Renaissance
Assertive Teaching	11/5/XX	2:30 p.m.	Van Gogh
Teacher Discipline	11/5/XX	4:00 p.m.	Italy Center

As always, I stand ready to assist you in making this school year a successful teaching experience.

Sincerely,

Lemmie Wade, PhD
Principal

Note: Include a copy of the convention booklet in the Unsatisfactory Teacher Evaluation Binder.

Section V—Videotapes to View

XYZ SCHOOL DISTRICT

ABC ELEMENTARY SCHOOL
1584 South Pine View Drive
Crescent Ridge, California 70799
(916) 444–4444

October 14, 20XX

Mr. William Anthony
ABC Elementary School

Dear Mr. Anthony:

Although you were previously given several suggestions to improve your teaching performance, I am providing you with a copy of the videotape series, *A Proactive Approach to Positive Classroom Management*, which shows successful classroom management techniques. I would like you to review these tapes and then meet with me to discuss the incorporation of these techniques into your classroom management. Please see my secretary to schedule a meeting with me.

Sincerely,

Lemmie Wade, PhD
Principal

Enclosure

Note: Include a copy of a description of the videotapes in the Unsatisfactory Teacher Evaluation Binder.

XYZ SCHOOL DISTRICT

ABC ELEMENTARY SCHOOL
1584 South Pine View Drive
Crescent Ridge, California 70799
(916) 444–4444

October 22, 20XX

Mr. William Anthony
ABC Elementary School

Dear Mr. Anthony:

As a resource for classroom teachers, a series of videotapes was recently purchased by our school district, which features Dr. Nikolus Jones, who is one of the leading experts in the field of education for teacher survival techniques. I feel that this series offers excellent information that should help you to become a more effective teacher. Therefore, I suggest that you view the following tapes in the school library within the next week:

1. *The Effective Teacher* (30 minutes)

2. *Lesson Planning* (25 minutes)

3. *Effective Classroom Management* (30 minutes)

4. *Classroom Rules and Procedures* (28 minutes)

5. *Key Instructional Behaviors* (35 minutes)

At our next postobservation conference, we will discuss the new strategies that you gleaned from these videotapes.

I stand ready to assist you in making this a successful school year.

Sincerely,

Lemmie Wade, PhD
Principal

Note: Include a copy of a description of the videotapes in the Unsatisfactory Teacher Evaluation Binder.

XYZ SCHOOL DISTRICT

ABC ELEMENTARY SCHOOL
1584 South Pine View Drive
Crescent Ridge, California 70799
(916) 444–4444

November 10, 20XX

Mr. William Anthony
ABC Elementary School

Dear Mr. Anthony:

I am providing you with the following videotapes, which demonstrate successful classroom management techniques:

- *Increasing Student Achievement Through Cooperative Learning*
- *Creating an Atmosphere for Positive Student Interaction*

I want you to view these tapes and then meet with me to discuss how you might incorporate these techniques into your classroom. Please see my secretary to schedule a meeting with me.

Sincerely,

Lemmie Wade, PhD
Principal

Enclosures

Note: Include a copy of a description of the videotapes in the Unsatisfactory Teacher Evaluation Binder.

XYZ SCHOOL DISTRICT

ABC ELEMENTARY SCHOOL
1584 South Pine View Drive
Crescent Ridge, California 70799
(916) 444–4444

December 8, 20XX

Mr. William Anthony
ABC Elementary School

Dear Mr. Anthony:

I am providing you the following videotapes, which demonstrate successful cooperative group learning techniques:

- *Structuring the Classroom Environment for Large Groups*
- *Small Group and Individualized Instruction*

I want you to view these tapes and then meet with me to discuss how you plan to incorporate these techniques into your classroom. Please see my secretary to schedule a meeting with me.

Sincerely,

Lemmie Wade, PhD
Principal

Enclosure

Note: Include a copy of a description of the videotapes in the Unsatisfactory Teacher Evaluation Binder.

Section V—Internet Sites to Search

XYZ SCHOOL DISTRICT

ABC ELEMENTARY SCHOOL
1584 South Pine View Drive
Crescent Ridge, California 70799
(916) 444–4444

October 22, 20XX

Mr. William Anthony
ABC Elementary School

Dear Mr. Anthony:

As you know, ABC Elementary School's Web page is connected to World Wide Web (www) sites to explore effective teaching strategies. In addition, you can connect to the district curriculum, which outlines effective lesson plans by grade level and subject area. I want you to explore the online curriculum as well as the following sites for great ideas to improve your teaching:

http://www.effectiveteaching.com

http://www.classroomdiscipline.com

http://www.assertivediscipline.com

http://www.modelsofdiscipline.com

http://www.whatgoodteachersdo.com

http://www.lessonplans.com

Sincerely,

Lemmie Wade, PhD
Principal

Note: Include a copy of a description of each Web site in the Unsatisfactory Teacher Evaluation Binder.

XYZ SCHOOL DISTRICT

ABC ELEMENTARY SCHOOL
1584 South Pine View Drive
Crescent Ridge, California 70799
(916) 444–4444

November 4, 20XX

Mr. William Anthony
ABC Elementary School

Dear Mr. Anthony:

I would like you to log on to the National Teacher Talk Web page at http://www
.teachertalk.com, which is specifically designed for new classroom teachers to
discuss and share classroom issues. This is an excellent site to obtain information about classroom instruction and classroom management. In addition,
the site offers message pages where you can leave specific questions for other
teachers to answer.

If you have any questions about accessing this Web site, please contact me.

Sincerely,

Lemmie Wade, PhD
Principal

Note: Include a copy of a description of the Web site in the Unsatisfactory Teacher
Evaluation Binder.

Section V—Order From Publisher's Catalog

XYZ SCHOOL DISTRICT

ABC ELEMENTARY SCHOOL
1584 South Pine View Drive
Crescent Ridge, California 70799
(916) 444–4444

October 18, 20XX

Mr. William Anthony
ABC Elementary School

Dear Mr. Anthony:

Enclosed is the 20XX Fast-Action Publishing Company catalog for teachers. All classroom teachers are allocated $50.00 each year to purchase improvement books. You may choose to use your allocation to order some books to help improve your teaching.

If you are interested in purchasing any of these books, please see my secretary for the order forms and then follow the procedures outlined in the Teacher Handbook.

Sincerely,

Lemmie Wade, PhD
Principal

Enclosure

Note: Include a copy of the catalog in the Unsatisfactory Teacher Evaluation Binder.

Section V—Read Weekly Bulletin

XYZ SCHOOL DISTRICT

ABC ELEMENTARY SCHOOL
1584 South Pine View Drive
Crescent Ridge, California 70799
(916) 444–4444

November 15, 20XX

Mr. William Anthony
ABC Elementary School

Dear Mr. Anthony:

As you know, the weekly staff bulletin contains information about daily school events for the next week as well as a listing of the upcoming school activities. A teacher checklist was added for all teachers (e.g., teachers are reminded to pick up their students on time and quietly escort them to their classrooms). I want you to reread the weekly bulletins for the months of September through November focusing on the teacher reminder section that may help you improve your teaching performance. In addition, all teachers receive in their e-mail inboxes the weekly staff bulletins.

Sincerely,

Lemmie Wade, PhD
Principal

Enclosures

Note: Include a copy of the weekly bulletins in the Unsatisfactory Teacher Evaluation Binder.

ABC ELEMENTARY SCHOOL
Weekly Bulletin
Week of September 6–10, 20XX

Good News Celebration!

The soccer team won this weekend
Happy Birthday Mrs. Jones, our engineer
Five teachers ran in the 5K Run at Lake Mead Park

Daily Actions

Monday, September 6

8:05 a.m.	New teacher meeting in conference room
9:00–9:10 a.m.	Classes delayed 10 minutes to take attendance
3:15 p.m.	Staff meeting in the library

Tuesday, September 7

8:05 a.m.	School council meeting in the library
3:00 p.m.	Debate club meeting in Room 36
3:30 p.m.	Dance troupe practice in the gym

Wednesday, September 8

Thursday, September 9

8:15 p.m.	School committee meetings in designated rooms

Friday, September 10

Payday

Reminders

Escort students to and from the cafeteria.
Review fire drill procedures in staff handbook.
Pick up children promptly after lunch.
Escort children to fire areas after school.
Classroom management plan due Wednesday by 3:30 p.m.

Looking Ahead to September

3:15 p.m. 9/14/XX (Tuesday) Staff meeting in the library
8:00 a.m. 9/16/XX (Thursday) New teacher meeting in Room 15
6:30 p.m. 9/21/XX (Tuesday) School Leadership Meeting in the library

---

Note: A copy of all weekly bulletins is included in the Unsatisfactory Teacher Evaluation Binder.

Section V—Explain Classroom Procedures

XYZ SCHOOL DISTRICT

ABC ELEMENTARY SCHOOL
1584 South Pine View Drive
Crescent Ridge, California 70799
(916) 444–4444

September 14, 20XX

Mr. William Anthony
ABC Elementary School

Dear Mr. Anthony:

After conducting several classroom observations, I am concerned about your apparent lack of classroom procedures. When I observed your classroom yesterday, students appeared to be unaware of classroom procedures. I want you to write out the following classroom procedures for your classroom:

I. Beginning Class

1. Taking and recording attendance
2. Tardiness
3. Providing academic warm-ups
4. Distributing materials
5. Beginning the lesson
6. Gaining student attention

II. Use of Classroom/School Areas

1. Drinks, bathroom, pencil sharpener
2. Learning centers
3. Storage areas

III. Work Requirement Procedures

1. Paper heading
2. Use of pen or pencil
3. Writing on the back of paper
4. Neatness/legibility
5. Incomplete work
6. Late work
7. Missed work
8. Independent work
9. Definition of "working alone"
10. Passing out books/supplies
11. Movement in and out of small groups

12. Expected behavior in groups
13. Out-of-seat policies
14. Conduct during interruptions
15. Homework assignments
16. Collecting assignments
17. Returning assignments
18. Posting student work
19. Rewards and incentives

You are to submit your classroom procedures by Friday, September 28, 20XX, at 3:00 p.m. Also, see my secretary to schedule a meeting within three days to discuss your classroom procedures in preparation for the next observation.

Sincerely,

Lemmie Wade, PhD
Principal

Note: Include a copy of the teacher's classroom procedures in the Unsatisfactory Teacher Evaluation Binder.

XYZ SCHOOL DISTRICT

ABC ELEMENTARY SCHOOL
1584 South Pine View Drive
Crescent Ridge, California 70799
(916) 444–4444

November 12, 20XX

Mr. William Anthony
ABC Elementary School

Dear Mr. Anthony:

In order to improve your teaching skills, I suggest that you focus on making improvements in the following specific performance areas:

Classroom organization and procedures
Physical organization
Expectations
Grading system
Learning environment
Positive teacher-student interaction
Rewards and encouragement
Multicultural awareness
Lesson planning and presentation
Introduction
Motivation
Organization
Closure
Assessment
Instructional techniques
Cooperative learning
Reading instruction
Mathematics instruction
Student discipline
Conflict resolution
Assertive discipline

I want to meet with you to discuss these improvement suggestions and the progress you believe that you have made to improve your teaching. Please see my secretary to schedule an appointment to discuss this letter.

Sincerely,

Lemmie Wade, PhD
Principal

Section VII—Discipline Referrals

XYZ SCHOOL DISTRICT

ABC ELEMENTARY SCHOOL
1584 South Pine View Drive
Crescent Ridge, California 70799
(916) 444–4444

This is a record of the students Mr. William Anthony sent to the office to receive disciplinary action from the school administrators:

Date	Time	Reasons for Discipline Referral
9–6–XX	9:25	Two students disrupt class by yelling and pounding.
9–6–XX	9:37	A student refuses to leave other children alone during reading class by yelling across the room.
9–6–XX	9:53	A student throws a pencil on floor and refuses to work.
9–6–XX	10:10	A student is in the hall without shoes kicking other children.
9–6–XX	10:30	A student is crawling around room and refusing to sit in assigned seat.
9–8–XX	10:25	A student is throwing paper on the floor and walking around the room. Stopping others from learning.
9–10–XX	None	A student is crawling on floor and using profane language.
9–10–XX	None	A student is throwing pencils on floor. Refuses to be quiet.
10–26–XX	None	A student refuses to line up to enter the building.
10–26–XX	1:30	A student is yelling during social studies.
11–5–XX	9:40	A student is yelling out during reading period.
11–5–XX	9:55	A student continues to disrupt class by walking around the room.
11–5–XX	11:10	A student is talking out in class.
11–5–XX	1:15	A student is yelling in class.
11–5–XX	1:45	A student is running, kicking, and throwing things in class.
11–8–XX	2:50	A student refuses to be quiet and work. Reading group cannot be conducted. Held with this disruption.
11–8–XX	2:50	A student is swearing in class.
11–9–XX	10:15	A student is throwing books around the room.

Date	Time	Reasons for Discipline Referral
11–9–XX	11:45	Two students are fighting in the classroom.
11–17–XX	11:15	A student is walking on top of tables and yelling in class.
12–6–XX	9:00	A student refuses to stop talking to other students who are trying to work.
12–6–XX	None	A student says his parents will call police, and he threatens to hit another student and the teacher. He yells across the room.
12–6–XX	None	A student has no supplies and throws materials borrowed from others onto the floor.
12–6–XX	None	Student throws pencil on floor. Sits in wrong seat. Refuses to work.
12–6–XX	9:50	A student is walking around the classroom.
12–6–XX	10:30	Two students are involved in a problem on the playground.
12–6–XX	10:55	A student kicked the classroom door.
12–6–XX	None	A student crawls around room. Refuses to sit or work at desk.
12–6–XX	None	A student is coloring paper on floor. Breaks pencils purposely. Walks around and refuses to sit. Prevents others from learning.
12–6–XX	None	A student is told to sit down more than three times. Crawls on floor. Bad language. Kicks.
12–6–XX	1:10	A student stole a pencil from another student.
12–6–XX	None	A student poses a safety hazard to other students.
12–6–XX	None	A student has a chronic lack of supplies. Throws crayons on floor. Told to be quiet four times and refuses.
12–10–XX	9:35	A student refuses to leave other students alone.
12–13–XX	10:15	A student yells across the room.
12–13–XX	10:20	A student has no supplies and throws loaned materials on the floor.
12–13–XX	11:10	A student throws pencil on floor. Sits in wrong seat. Refuses to work.
12–14–XX	1:15	A student refuses to come from the playground with supplies.
12–15–XX	11:30	A student kicked the wall.

Date	Time	Reasons for Discipline Referral
12–16–XX	1:00	This student needs a break.
12–17–XX	1:25	An aide left two students alone in room 27.
12–18–XX	1:50	A student crawls around room. Refuses to sit or work on easiest tasks. things. Daily, hourly disruption.
12–20–XX	10:30	A student calls out in class. Throws crayons.
1–5–XX	10:00	A student throws coloring paper on floor. Breaks pencils purposely. Walks around and refuses to sit. Prevents others from learning.
1–10–XX	2:15	A student is told to sit down more than three times. Crawls on floor. Bad language to Kicks.
1–21–XX	11:40	A student stole a pencil.
1–24–XX	9:35	A student poses a safety hazard to other students.
1–24–XX	11:00	A student has a chronic lack of supplies. Throws crayons on floor. Told to be quiet four times and refuses.
1–24–XX	1:30	A student says shut up to the teacher.
2–4–XX	9:15	A student refuses to sit and be quiet and work. Uncooperative.
2–4–XX	9:50	A student needs a break.
2–4–XX	10:15	A student refuses to work. Throws work on floor. Crawls on floor. 45 worksheets stapled to this.
2–4–XX	10:20	A student refuses to sit, be quiet, and work.
2–4–XX	10:55	A student refuses to cooperate. Very loud. Won't sit down. out papers. Uses foul language (dick, gay, homo). A regular circus clown. Thinks she's very funny.
2–4–XX	11:10	A student throws crayons. Refuses to cooperate with teacher.
2–4–XX	None	A student entered building at 12:50. Hit several students despite being told to sit down. to keep her hands to herself. Tipped her chair over. Refused to settle down.
2–4–XX	1:00	A student is a safety hazard. Throws crayons.
2–4–XX	1:45	A student walked across the room and hit the wall.
2–4–XX	2:25	A student used inappropriate language (kiss your mother's wiener) to another child. Scribbles on
2–4–XX	2:50	A student calls out. Doesn't work.
2–4–XX	2:50	A student hit some girls.

Date	Time	Reasons for Discipline Referral
2–7–XX	9:30	A student yells across room.
2–7–XX	11:15	A student kicks the desk of others.
2–8–XX	1:12	A student tries walk around the room.
2–9–XX	9:20	A student told to do own work. Refuses. Refuses to leave and alone.
2–9–XX	10:05	A student refuses to keep reader open. Does not want to learn to read.
2–9–XX	11:15	A student has no crayons, erasers. No effort to work.
2–10–XX	11:05	A student ran down hall. Didn't go to toilet. Disobedient. Disrupts class. constantly. Put plastic bag over her head.
2–14–XX	11:05	A student had difficulty learning tens in math with the rest of the class.
2–14–XX	1:30	A student yelled, threw her paper on the floor, and crayons. Refused to settle down.
2–15–XX	1:30	A student hit and kicked. Yells out.
2–16–XX	2:00	A student prevents the class from learning to read. Disrespectful.
2–21–XX	1:30	A student repeatedly told to work. Continues to talk across room. and does not work. Prevents education and reading groups from operating.
2–23–XX	None	A student prevents reading work of class being improved. Gets up without permission and disrupts the reading lesson. and rips work.
2–23–XX	9:15	A student does not do what the teacher asks.
2–24–XX	9:45	A student ran and kicked.
2–25–XX	10:45	A student refuses to write lines. Throws pencil on floor.
3–1–XX	11:30	A student yells loudly. Refuses to listen to art teacher. Disrespectful.
3–2–XX	10:20	A student refuses to be quiet and work. Kicks desks.
3–3–XX	9:00	A student is disruptive. Teacher says he cannot teach with her in class.
3–3–XX	9:30	A student is rude. Does not demonstrate Kindergarten readiness. Does not work. disrupter. Kicking still. Steals 's eraser.
3–5–XX	10:30	A student's parent disrupts class.
3–6–XX	11:00	A student is unruly. Please remove him.

Date	Time	Reasons for Discipline Referral
3–7–XX	3:30	A student is not respectful to teacher.
3–21–XX	11:35	A student returned at 11:30 from the office. Not ready for class. Belligerent still.
3–21–XX	2:05	A student calls out. Jumps out of seat to hit two desks.
3–28–XX	9:50	A student creates constant noise. Prevents education of class.
3–31–XX	11:04	A student prevents p.m. reading groups. Yells out. Talks. Told to be quiet four times.
4–1–XX	1:30	A student is a p.m. reading group disrupter. Loud, rude when not reading aloud. chosen to go with tutor.
4–2–XX	2:13	A student's parent disrupts class.
4–4–XX	9:15	At 9:10, the student had some candy stolen by someone in Room 30.
4–5–XX	2:00	A student is upset and uncooperative all day.
4–9–XX	1:15	A student refuses to settle down after lunch.

Section VIII—Letters Informing the Teacher About Parental Complaints

XYZ SCHOOL DISTRICT

ABC ELEMENTARY SCHOOL
1584 South Pine View Drive
Crescent Ridge, California 70799
(916) 444–4444

During the 20XX–20XX school year, parental complaints were filed at ABC Elementary School against William Anthony. These 23 parental complaints were related to how Mr. Anthony's teaching performance negatively affected their children's education. The XYZ School District's contractual procedures were followed to resolve these parental complaints. At this time, I will give you an overview of the parental complaints, including letters, telephone class, and e-mail messages.

XYZ SCHOOL DISTRICT

ABC ELEMENTARY SCHOOL
1584 South Pine View Drive
Crescent Ridge, California 70799
(916) 444–4444

September 10, 20XX

Mr. William Anthony
ABC Elementary School

Dear Mr. Anthony:

Part III, Section A, of the XYZ contract states when parental or public complaints are filed against the teacher, he or she must be made aware of the criticism. Therefore, I am forwarding the attached parental complaint form received about you on September 9, 20XX.

I want you to meet with me in my office on September 12, 20XX, at 3:15 p.m. to discuss this parental complaint. If this time is inconvenient, please contact my secretary to reschedule the meeting immediately in order to resolve this complaint by September 15, 20XX.

Sincerely,

Lemmie Wade, PhD
Principal

Enclosure

Section VIII—Parental Complaints Filed Against the Teacher

Parental Complaint Form

Date _____   Time _____ a.m./p.m.

Student _____   Grade _____   ID Number _____

Address _____

Person Filing Complaint _____

Relationship to Student _____

Phone Number: Home _____   Other _____   E-mail _____

Nature of Compliant _____

_____

_____

Action Requested _____

_____

Has a Previous Complaint Been Filed? Yes _____ No _____ Dates _____

Person(s) Spoken with: _____

_____
Name/Title/Department

_____
Name/Title/Department

Resolution _____

_____

_____

_____

Complaint Resolved _____   Further Action Necessary _____

_____
Signature/Title/Department

Parental Complaint Letter

September 15, 20XX

Dear Mrs. Wade, Principal:

I am writing this letter to express my concern about the safety of my son in Mr. Anthony's room.

My son told me students are being hit in the head with flying objects constantly. In fact, my son was hit three times with pencils and once with a wood cube. On one day, one child was imitating a TV wrestler and tried to choke my son in front of Mr. Anthony, and he did nothing. My son told me that scissors are thrown across the room quite often and spitballs fly regularly.

My son comes home with headaches caused by stress and the noise in the classroom, and he doesn't want to go back to school anymore. I am afraid for my son's safety as well as the safety of the other children in Mr. Anthony's classroom. I believe that my son is not getting a good education. I am requesting that he be assigned immediately to Mr. Patterson's class before he gets hurt in Mr. Anthony's classroom.

Sincerely,

Mrs. Johnson

Parental Complaint Letter

September 15, 20XX

To Whom It May Concern:

I am afraid for my daughter Judy, who is in Mr. Anthony's classroom. My daughter is afraid of being hit with spitballs, crayons, and other flying objects in the classroom. She says that Mr. Anthony stands in front of the classroom and doesn't pay attention to the bad children throwing things. She also says that her school supplies (paper, pencils, pens, markers, and crayons) have been stolen out of her desk. Judy does not want to go back to Mr. Anthony's classroom.

Sincerely,

Mrs. Reyes

Parental Complaint Letter

September 27, 20XX

Mrs. Wade,

Are the children out of control in Room 214? My son Johnny says his classroom is out of control, and no learning is taking place. If this is true, I want him transferred to another classroom immediately. Johnny also says that Mr. Anthony doesn't have any control over the children. He does not want to go back to school if he has to be in Mr. Anthony's classroom.

Please call me at 775–8339 to let me know about your decision to transfer my son to another classroom. I want to hear from you by the end of this week, or I will take this to the media. I want something done.

Sincerely,

Mr. John Zebelle, Sr.

Section VIII—Phone and E-mail Messages

Phone Message

ABC ELEMENTARY SCHOOL

To: Dr. Wade

Date: 9/17/20XX

Time: 11:45 a.m.

While you were out

Mrs. Beverly Rodriguez
Parent of Javiera

Phone 897–4000 Ex. 35

- ☐ Telephoned
- ☐ Came to see you
- ☐ Wants to see you
- ☐ Please call him/her
- ☐ Will call again
- ☑ Urgent
- ☐ Returned your call

Message Re: Mr. Anthony's classroom.
Wants her son transferred to another room.

Phone Message

ABC ELEMENTARY SCHOOL

To: Dr. Wade

Date: 10/7/20XX

Time: 10:30 a.m. and 2:30 p.m.

While you were out

Mr. and Mrs. Simmons
Parents of Daryl

Phone 303–9399

- ☐ Telephoned
- ☐ Came to see you
- ☑ Wants to see you
- ☐ Please call him/her
- ☐ Will call again
- ☐ Urgent
- ☐ Returned your call

Message Re: Mr. Anthony's classroom.
Wants their daughter transferred to another room.
This is the second message.

Phone Message

ABC ELEMENTARY SCHOOL

To: Dr. Wade
Date: 10/7/20XX
Time: 10:30 a.m. and 2:30 p.m.

While you were out
Ms. Henderson, parental complaint center

Phone 444-9705

- ☐ Telephoned
- ☐ Came to see you
- ☐ Wants to see you
- ☐ Please call him/her
- ☐ Will call again
- ☐ Urgent
- ☑ Returned your call

Message Mr. and Mrs. Simmons. They are complaining about a teacher at school—Mr. Anthony.

E-mail Message

E-mail:	**ABCelementaryschool.XYZ.edu**
Date:	November 1, 20XX
To:	Dr. Wade
Cc:	Superintendent of Schools and my attorney
Subject:	Mr. Anthony's Classroom
From:	GoldenB@butterfly.com

I am concerned about the education my daughter is receiving in Mr. Anthony's classroom. She said that the class is too noisy for learning to take place. She also said that kids are walking around the room, throwing spitballs, and the teacher does nothing. I went to the class today at 9:30 a.m. and found it to be a terrible place. Nobody can learn in that class. I want my daughter taken out of his class immediately.

Please e-mail or call me to let me know when my child will be transferred to another room.

E-mail Message

E-mail:	**ABCelementaryschool.XYZ.edu**
Date:	November 17, 20XX
To:	Dr. Wade
Cc:	Superintendent of Schools
Subject:	Transfer my Child!
From:	The Rev. Arthur H. Anderson

Good Heavens, what in the world is going on in Mr. Anthony's classroom?

I am displeased and want a room change for my son. Why is my son suffering in the classroom? What do you plan to do about this classroom? The education of my son will **not** suffer because of this teacher. My son must be moved to another room, or he will for sure fail the state test to move to the next grade.

Thank you

E-mail Message

E-mail: **ABCelementaryschool.XYZ.edu**

Date: October 21, 20XX

To: Dr. Wade

Cc: Superintendent of Schools

Subject: Transfer my Child!

From: Lorraine Tillman

What a disappointment for my child to be in Mr. Anthony's classroom. He has absolutely no control over those students—how can they be learning anything? Those 30 students will not get a good education. What can be done to get my child into another classroom? Please e-mail me about the room change immediately.

Section IX—Work Samples

XYZ SCHOOL DISTRICT   ABC ELEMENTARY SCHOOL
                                       1584 South Pine View Drive
                                       Crescent Ridge, California 70799
                                       (916) 444–4444

The XYZ School District has set curriculum goals for each grade step. Despite efforts to get Mr. Anthony to follow the set curriculum, he did not follow the curriculum as mandated by the school committee as well as the state department of education. Attached are student work samples given to students by Mr. William Anthony.

References

Acheson, Keith A., & Gall, M. D. (2002). *Clinical supervision and teacher development: Preservice and inservice applications* (5th ed.). New York: Wiley.

Downey, C. J., Steffy, B. E., English, F. W., Frase, L. E., & Poston, W. K., Jr. (2004). *The three-minute classroom walk-through*. Thousand Oaks, CA: Corwin.

Essex, N. L. (2004). *School law and the public schools: A practical guide for educational leaders* (3rd ed.). Allyn & Bacon.

LaMorte, M. W. (2002). *School law cases and concepts*. Boston: Allyn & Bacon.

Lawrence, C., & Vachon, M. (1997). *The incompetent specialist: How to evaluate, document performance, and dismiss school staff*. Thousand Oaks, CA: Corwin.

Lawrence, C., & Vachon, M. (2003). *How to handle staff misconduct: A step-by-step guide* (2nd ed.). Thousand Oaks, CA: Corwin.

Valente, W. D. (2000). *Education law: Public and private* (Volume 1, Sections 1.1–16). St. Paul, MN: West Publishing.

Suggested Web Sites

http://www.educationnews.org

http://www.educationweek.org

http://www.teacher.com/sdoe.htm

Index

NOTE: Page numbers in italics refer to figures.

**CORWIN
PRESS**

The Corwin Press logo—a raven striding across an open book—represents the union of courage and learning. Corwin Press is committed to improving education for all learners by publishing books and other professional development resources for those serving the field of K–12 education. By providing practical, hands-on materials, Corwin Press continues to carry out the promise of its motto: **"Helping Educators Do Their Work Better."**